RATH

Established 1742

THE

BONES

STORY OF RATHBONES

SINCE 1742

Copyright © Rathbone Brothers Plc 2008

First published 2008 by James & James (Publishers) Ltd
a subsidiary of Third Millenium Information Ltd
2–5 Benjamin Street, London EC1M 5QL, United Kingdom

www/tmltd.com

ISBN-978 1 903942 93 2

Published by James & James (Publishing) Ltd
A subsidiary of Third Millennium Information Ltd

Designed by Matthew Wilson and John Rice
Project management and picture research by Susan Millership
Photography by Charles Best
Production by Bonnie Murray

Reprographics by Studio Fasoli, Italy
Printed and bound by Gorenjski Tisk, Slovenia

Contents

Foreword

The quarter of a century since 'Big Bang' has seen an extraordinary transformation in the financial services industry in the UK.

David Lascelles's engaging and sensitively written history of Rathbones skillfully sets out the long history of the business in the context of social and economic changes exploring the transformation of a 17th-century trading house into the modern Rathbones, a provider of investment management and trust and tax services to wealthy private individuals and trustees.

The book sheds some fascinating light on both the extraordinary range of interests and achievements of the extended Rathbone family, and on the history of the city of Liverpool in particular.

For those of us who work in Rathbones in the 21st century the book is a timely, if sometimes intimidating, reminder of the remarkable inheritance which is in our trust.

Mark Powell *chairman*
June 2008

Merseyside to Mayfair

Rathbone Brothers officially dates its birth to 1742 because that is the first year for which business records survive. But this is slightly modest. There is good evidence that Rathbones was trading well before that date, and the family origins of the firm go back far into the 1600s. This means that by 2008 Rathbones had been in existence for nearly 300 years, a remarkable achievement which puts it on a par with eminent institutions such as Hoares Bank (founded in 1672), Barclays (1690), Coutts Bank (1692) and the Bank of England (1694). Barings – a firm which had close links with Rathbones – only came into existence in 1762, and failed to stay the course. Rothschilds founded its London office in 1810, by which time Rathbones had been going for several generations. All the other famous financial

names came much later.

It is always fascinating to ask what enables businesses to flourish over such great lengths of time: strong genes, good fortune, the right connections, a nose for opportunity… All these played their part in the story of Rathbones since its humble beginnings as a Liverpool timber yard. The family genes fluctuated: some generations did better than others, but all managed to keep the business going through tumultuous periods in British history. Good fortune played its part as well, not least because Rathbones, like many Liverpool merchants in Georgian and Victorian times, did well out of wars. Good connections and a keen business instinct were also Rathbone strengths; no one dealing in the vast array of

merchant markets could have survived without them. At one period, Rathbones was dealing simultaneously in indigo, rice, butter and mahogany, making prices for each, and was active on four continents.

But while the persistence of good traits through successive generations is central to the Rathbones story, so is change. Rathbones would have gone the way of Barings more than a century ago had it not been for a readiness to adapt. From its beginnings as a sawing business, Rathbones became progressively a timber merchant, a shipbuilder, a general merchant, a commodity dealer, a shipping company, a manager of family funds and now a wealth manager in its own right. Each of these changes was driven by the knowledge that

failure to move on would mean certain death. Rathbones has also taken many forms: partnerships, alliances, private limited company and now plc, all of which required an adaptive spirit and an eye for the greater purpose of profitable survival. In the process, it expanded from Merseyside to Mayfair in the heart of London, where it is now headquartered.

But while Rathbones' record is impressive and provides the firm with a distinctive culture, is it enough in a ferociously competitive world where the future, not the past, is what counts? The story that follows should help supply the answer.

David Lascelles

Rathbones' London office is in the heart of Mayfair on New Bond Street.

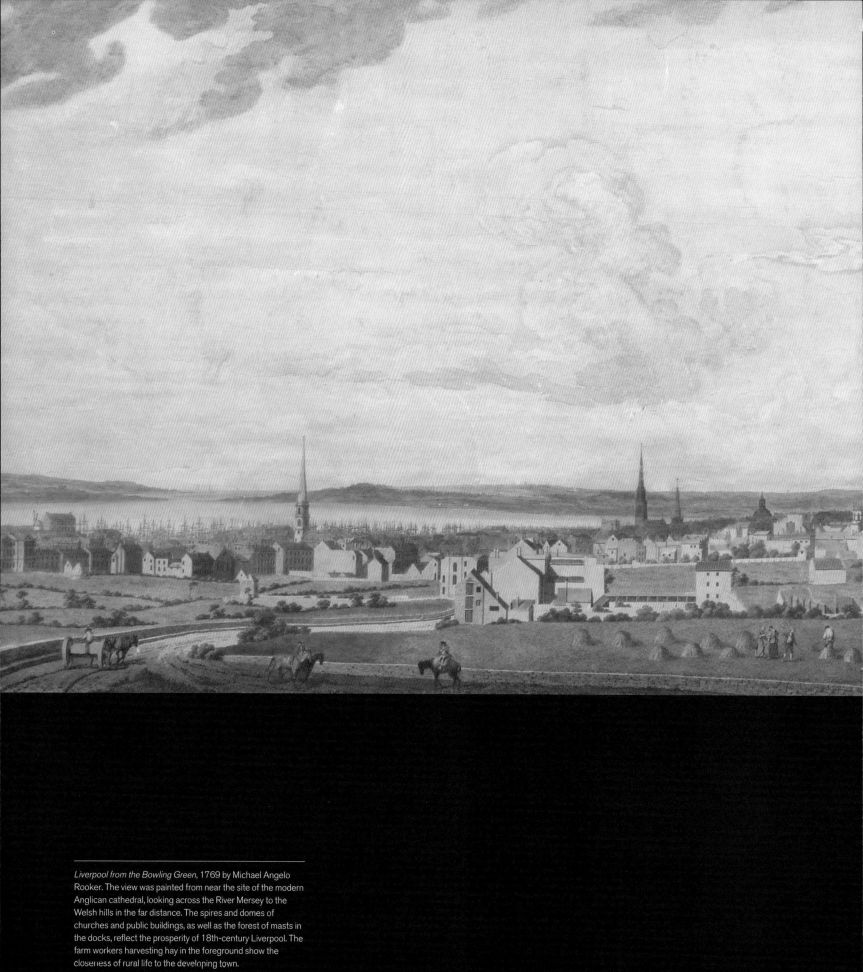

Liverpool from the Bowling Green, 1769 by Michael Angelo Rooker. The view was painted from near the site of the modern Anglican cathedral, looking across the River Mersey to the Welsh hills in the far distance. The spires and domes of churches and public buildings, as well as the forest of masts in the docks, reflect the prosperity of 18th-century Liverpool. The farm workers harvesting hay in the foreground show the closeness of rural life to the developing town.

1

BEGINNINGS
1669–1750

Around the year 1720 a young farmer's son set out from the north Cheshire village of Gawsworth to go to Liverpool. The distance was only 40 miles, but it would have been a difficult journey, particularly if he had to walk, which is likely. The roads were poor, and Liverpool itself was isolated on a muddy stretch of the Mersey's north shore and could not be reached by coach.

But we know that he arrived safely because he was William Rathbone who went on to found the Rathbone family business and the dynasty which ran it for over 200 years.

He was not the first William Rathbone: his forebears had lived in Cheshire for hundreds of years, and two of them were mayors of Chester in the 1500s. The earliest Rathbone in this history is William's father, known as 'the first', who was born in Gawsworth in 1669 and became a yeoman farmer. In 1688, when he was 19, he married a lady called Martha Vigour who lived up to her splendid name by bearing him eleven children, of whom five sons and two daughters survived to adulthood. Among those who died as infants were two boys, both of whom were named William. The Rathbone couple

clearly wanted to name an heir after his father, and it must have been with much joy that Martha produced another son, her fifth, in 1696, whom they also named William. He survived, and history has come to call him William II.

The young William was about 25 when he left home. We don't know why he went. Perhaps he did not want to spend the rest of his life on a farm. Gawsworth then, as now, lies in a quiet corner of Cheshire and would have been little touched by the great industrial stirrings of the age, even by the South Sea Bubble which burst in 1720 and ruined thousands. William's father's will, drawn up in 1741, gives us an idea of the modesty of the Rathbone household. His possessions included a few sticks of furniture, a feather bed, a ladder, 'a muck

The earliest known painting of Liverpool, 1680. With trade booming, the river is teeming with local craft and ocean-going vessels.

Where it all began

Gawsworth, the village from which William Rathbone II set out to make his fortune in the 1720s, is still to be found in a rural stretch of the north-west Cheshire Plain where it meets the Pennine foothills. But a typical village it is not. There is no high street or cluster of country cottages. Instead, Gawsworth comprises a remarkable set of handsome period houses grouped in spacious grounds around a string of artificial lakes, or fisheries. The fine crenellated tower of the church of St James the Great provides the backdrop to a scene created by the efforts – and wealth –

of man rather than nature. The main house, Gawsworth Hall, a splendid black and white mansion in the herringbone Cheshire style, was the 16th-century home of Mary Fitton, reputedly the 'Dark Lady' of Shakespeare's sonnets.

Exactly where William Rathbone I lived is not known, but there is still plenty of evidence of his clan: the church register tells us that many Rathbones rest in the graveyard – including William's brother David, and more Rathbones appear on a list of churchwardens on the nave wall.

This part of rural Cheshire still is Rathbone country. At the nearby village of Rainow the vicar today is the Rev. Steve Rathbone, who is descended from 'the Rathbones who stayed behind'. The Rev. Rathbone has followed the fortunes of the Rathbones business, and says he feels 'a sense of pride' in the family dynasty.

cart… and… an old broken marl cart', worth a total of £25. The most precious items in the will were eight cows and two 'twinters' (calves who have lived through two winters) valued at £18.

If it was entrepreneurial zeal which took William II away, why Liverpool? Macclesfield just up the road had the beginnings of a textile industry and would soon become Britain's biggest silk producer; plenty of opportunities there for an enterprising young man. There is evidence to suggest that the Gawsworth Rathbones were in the wood business, and that William II saw an opportunity in shipbuilding. His elder brother David, who is buried in Gawsworth churchyard, is described as a carpenter on his tombstone. If so, he might have done better

to head for Chester, a shipping centre that was much easier to reach than Liverpool and twice the size.

But Liverpool it was. One possibility is that William had relations who enticed him over. A modern-day Rathbone, Joy Robinson, says in her history of the family that there existed a Rathbone line in Liverpool who were William's cousins. However, it would be right to credit him with identifying Liverpool as the town of the future, the sort of place where an ambitious young man could get in on the ground floor and make a real fortune rather than, as would be the case at Chester, compete with dozens of long-established businesses. Liverpool certainly had a growing reputation at the time: apprentice records for the first half of the 18th century show that young people were moving in in large numbers from the surrounding countryside, Lancashire, Cheshire and North Wales, even Ireland, drawn by the buzz of a new port. Four out of five Liverpudlians were incomers.

Even so, Liverpool in 1720 cannot have been a particularly prepossessing place, even by the standards of the age. Daniel Defoe, who visited it in 1680, gave it an upbeat report: it was 'a large, handsome, well built and increasing and thriving town'. But later descriptions dwell on the fact that it was small and cut off, that its population of around 10,000 lived in low brick houses clustered along narrow streets 'without the charms of shape, colour or carving'. On its southern rim there was the windswept Mersey, which provided most Liverpudlians with their living, to the north empty moorland. Industrious, certainly, but probably chill and lonely for a young man who had just left home. It must also have been a rough place, the gathering ground of sailors, privateers and smugglers. Bryan Blundell, who was mayor in the early 1700s, kept a diary from which we learn that public drunkenness and brothels were a constant threat to morality and public order. To suppress them, he ordered his craftsmen to build a ducking chair, a cage capable of holding a dozen people, and a new pair of stocks. Into these went 'the people who was taken in the night at all disorderly houses and in wicked practices'. Blundell reports with satisfaction that his measures 'struck such terror amongst them that many of these common strumpets quitted the town, being so disturbed in their trade of wickedness, and fled to other parts where they was in hopes to go on in the old way without such disturbances'.

William would have needed courage and imagination to believe that this lonely riverside community had great prospects, but these were precisely the qualities that generations of Rathbones were to display.

Liverpool did, however, have one big thing going for it: a dock. People originally settled here because of a small creek in the river bank which offered shelter from the Mersey's tidal waters; this was probably the lither (dull or muddy) pool that gave the town its

A view of Liverpool from across the River Mersey in 1728. The first dock can be seen on the right, surrounded by small businesses such as glass-making, sugar-baking and shipbuilding. The ships out of the water further to the right are where Rathbones later had its timber yard.

Vol I. page 378

J. Ryland del. et sculp.

uth West View of Liverpool.

A page from the Rathbones' Day Book. Rathbones dates its foundation to 1742, the start of the Day Book that shows that William Rathbone II was running a busy timber yard.

berthing facilities of more fortunate natural harbours like London and Bristol.

In 1709 the town fathers took the enormously bold decision to build what was to become the first commercial wet dock in the world: an enclosed basin with heavy doors which could be swung shut to retain water at low tide. Although Liverpool employed an experienced engineer, Thomas Steers, who was familiar with Dutch lock-building techniques, it was not easy. The initial costing was £6,000, but within five years this had doubled and nearly bankrupted Liverpool. The town was only bailed out by wealthy well-wishers. But the great project succeeded. Steers was feted and went on to become mayor.

The dock was finally completed in 1715, and transformed Liverpool's fortunes. Much larger ships could now transfer their cargoes without being delayed by the tides. It was a momentous coming-together of the 'entrepreneurial flair, embryonic civic pride, political skill and self-interest' for which Liverpool was to become famous. By the time William II arrived in the 1720s, Liverpool's shipping industry was in the early stages of a boom. The number of locally-owned ships had doubled to more than 100 since work on the dock started. Alongside shipping, service industries were getting going as well: shipbuilding and repair, warehousing, merchanting, sailmaking and ropemaking.

William II had chosen the right destination and timed it well. He began his business as a sawyer but quickly expanded to become a timber merchant, a shipbuilder and eventually a shipowner in his own right. In 1730, we learn from a deed of apprenticeship that he teamed up with a certain Richard Rutter, whose family was to have close links with the Rathbones for several generations. Two years later, William II acquired a lease on a property in Hanover Street, the town's main thoroughfare leading down to the new dock, and in 1741 he took on a second property in adjoining Duke Street, pointers that the business was doing well.

It is in the following year, 1742, that we start to get a more detailed picture of the Rathbones' business thanks to a surviving Day Book, a magnificent leather-bound ledger of 540 pages which lists the firm's daily incomings and outgoings for the next five years. Since this is the earliest formal record of the business, today's Rathbones dates its foundation

name. (This is but one of many theories about the origin of Liverpool's name.) The Mersey's tides are ferocious: they race in at high speed and raise the water level by 30 feet, so any protection is welcome. But as shipping grew in the late 1600s and early 1700s the pool became inadequate; Liverpool needed a place where ships could moor regardless of the state of the tide. Its future depended on it: new trade routes were opening up around Europe and the Mediterranean, but also to the East, Africa and America, and the ambitious young port would miss out on these opportunities unless it could match the to 1742, though, as we have seen, there is evidence that it started several years earlier.

From the Day Book we deduce that William II was running a busy little timber yard employing as many as a dozen people, most of them sawyers. One of the earliest entries informs us that Thos. Willson earned two shillings and four pence for 'one day's work sawing oak'. William also trades in English fir, walnut and mahogany, which he delivers in the form of balks (rafters), planks and 'cuts'. References to masts and 'dales' (wooden pipes) tell us that much of this commerce was with the shipbuilding trade, and probably opened the way to William's own entry into the business. We learn from the book of the existence of a ship called *Elizabeth Rathbone*, which he probably owned since both his second wife and his daughter had that name. How far the Rathbones' shipping interests extended is hard to say. There are a number of poorly documented references to between four and six small vessels either owned or hired by the family, which traded with the American eastern seaboard, importing timber.

In 1722 William II married a girl called Sarah Hyde who came from Walton-on-the-Hill, a parish in the south east of Liverpool. This is one of the dates that helps us to establish when William arrived on Merseyside. Sarah bore him three children, including a son in 1726 who was to become William III. Unfortunately, she died two years later aged only 26. Three years later, in 1731, William II married again. His second wife, Elizabeth Shepherd, bore him three children, including young Elizabeth and a son, Joseph, whose misfortune it is that his school bills have survived, showing that his parents had to spend large amounts of money on repairs for his clothes and shoes. Joseph went on to play an important role in cementing the Rathbones into the Quaker business community by marrying Mary Darby, the daughter of Abraham Darby, one of the fathers of the Industrial Revolution who owned the Coalbrookdale Iron-works in Shropshire, in which the Rathbones were also to acquire an interest.

The year 1731 is another landmark because this was when William II became a Quaker, a step which appears to have had a dual motivation. One was that his father had become a Quaker a few years earlier, the other was that Elizabeth was a Quaker and would, by the rules of her sect, only be allowed to marry another Quaker. William's conversion would

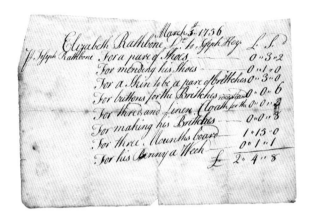

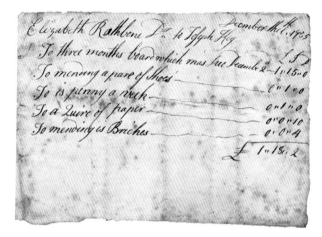

Joseph Rathbone's school bills.

establish a tradition of non-conformism and philanthropy that became a hallmark of the Rathbone family and business. William may also have taken this step at the urging of Richard Rutter, who belonged to a family with strong Quaker traditions. Ten years later, in 1741, William II was asked to oversee the refurbishment of the Liverpool Quakers' meeting house in Hackins Hey, and contributed generously to the cost. When he died 'of a fever' five years later in 1746, he was buried there. Subsequently, his second daughter Penelope took over the management of Hackins Hey and 'busied herself with soup kitchens and other efforts to relieve the ever-present misery of the poor of Liverpool'.

Thus was the Rathbones' business born. William may have counted himself among the poor of Liverpool when he arrived, but by the time of his death, Rathbones was a flourishing timber trading business with growing connections at home and overseas, and the family itself was comfortably off. In the best dynastic tradition, he also left a capable heir to carry it on.

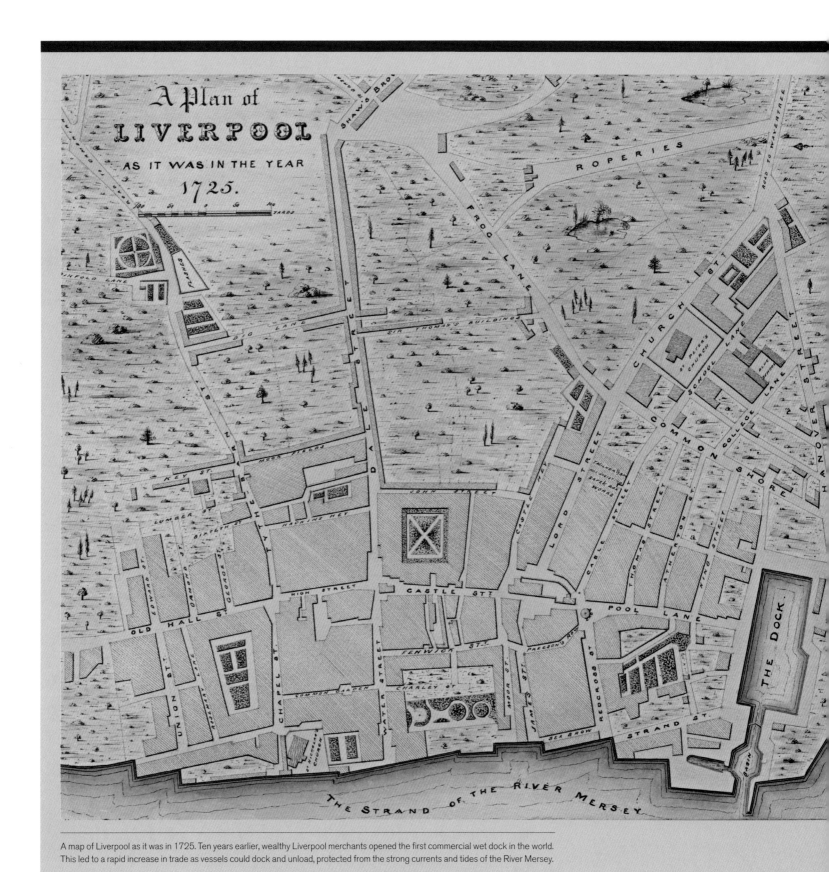

A map of Liverpool as it was in 1725. Ten years earlier, wealthy Liverpool merchants opened the first commercial wet dock in the world. This led to a rapid increase in trade as vessels could dock and unload, protected from the strong currents and tides of the River Mersey.

Liverpool the unstoppable

The port that William II found when he arrived in Liverpool in the 1720s would have been small but bustling – a promising place for an ambitious young man.

Liverpool had already been in the shipping business for 100 years, but in a limited way. Its position on the north-west coast of England was far from ideal in the 1600s, remote from the trade routes of the English Channel and the markets of Continental Europe. Much of its early trade consisted of shipping out Cheshire salt and Lancashire coal, and importing flax from Ireland for Manchester's early textile industry. Its other role was to act as a staging post for shipping between the Channel and Scotland or Ireland.

But the development of the Americas and the West Indies in the 17th century changed all that. Suddenly, Liverpool found itself on the right side of the British Isles, and its enterprising merchants opened up a brisk trade in New World commodities, mainly tobacco and sugar. By the end of the 1600s, Liverpool's waterfront boasted several sugar refineries, a salt refinery, the largest tobacco warehouse in England and its own customs house, which freed it from customs control in the rival port of Chester. The outbreak of hostilities between Britain and the Continent in the early 1700s (the Marlborough wars) also drove shipping away from England's southern ports into the safer reaches of the Irish Sea, bringing more business Liverpool's way.

The only big setback Liverpool suffered around this time was when Glasgow seized the opportunity of Scotland's union with England in 1707 to snatch away its tobacco business by offering cheaper and faster links to the Virginia plantations, an indication of how hotly Britain's ports competed with each other.

It was a blow, but by then, Liverpool's other interests were booming. On the import side, sugar soared and was enormously profitable: refined sugar sold on the Liverpool dockside for four times the price paid for it in Barbados. The improvement of navigation to Manchester made Liverpool the natural offloading point for the growing trade in West Indian cotton. Like Bristol, it also developed a brisk business in wines from Bordeaux, Spain and Portugal.

On the outgoing side, salt and coal remained staples, but Liverpool now saw a swelling flow of manufactured goods from the English heartland – textiles from Manchester, ironware from Birmingham and pottery from Staffordshire where Wedgwood opened his first works in 1759. Liverpool also became the natural departure point for emigration to the colonies of New England – the start of a flourishing passenger business.

The most obvious sign of Liverpool's growing success was its adoption of plans in 1737 to build a second wet dock, twice as large as the first, costing £14,000, a project which once again nearly bankrupted the town and only succeeded after much delay. But this facility, the Salthouse Dock, was vital to the port's future. There were now around 200 locally owned vessels, and the number of ships calling at Liverpool was running at several hundred a year, more than a third from outside British waters, mainly the Baltic and the Americas, carrying a huge array of goods from the humdrum to the obscure. In 1736–37 more than 1,000 tons of cheese passed through Liverpool's docks, this 200 years before the days of refrigerated transport.

By the middle of the 18th century, Liverpool was well on its way to becoming one of the leading ports in the British Isles. Two of its main rivals had their problems: Chester, 20 miles up the River Dee, was silting up, and Whitehaven up in Cumberland had coal to export but no hinterland to absorb imports. One of Liverpool's advantages, despite its remoteness, was good communication with industry. The Mersey and the Weaver connected the city with regional manufacturing centres and, as the 18th century progressed, canals – many financed by Liverpool capital – extended the port's reach far inland, eventually to Leeds on the far side of the Pennines. Even Bristol, Liverpool's main west coast rival, could not keep up, and was forced to yield its position as Britain's second port to Merseyside around 1770.

In his chronicle of the Rathbone family, the 19th-century MP Augustine Birrell lists three 'permanent factors' behind Liverpool's greatness.

'First, the marvellous rise and (despite the black smoke, the tall chimneys and the poisoned rivers) romantic growth of the manufacturing districts of Lancashire; and Second, the peopling of America with men of our own race and speech, and Third, the acquisition of our Colonies in the West Indies.'

He might have added the single-mindedness of its citizens. Everyone in Liverpool was determined that the port should succeed, from its town council which consisted almost entirely of shipowners and merchants, to the growing crowds of immigrants who came to find a new life. But there was a dark side to this tale of unstoppable prosperity – slavery – which we shall come to in the next chapter.

2

THE MERCHANT
ON MERSEYSIDE 1750–1790

William Rathbone III, who took over the business when his father died in 1746, is the first 'WR' to emerge as a rounded character in the Rathbones story. For a start, there is a portrait, a pen drawing of him in middle age, showing a stern face in profile, thickset and bewigged, seemingly lacking mirth or warmth, inscribed nonetheless with the words 'Thy Affectionate Father Wm Rathbone'. There are also descriptions of him by others, and there are his letters which document the strong growth that Rathbones enjoyed under his leadership. All this leads us to rate him as one of the key characters in the early phase of the business, a man of confidence, energy and shrewdness who transformed Rathbones into one of the largest and most successful merchanting businesses on the Liverpool waterfront.

One fact we know about William III before he even came to head the family firm is that he very nearly did not. The Day Book shows that he had been working as an apprentice for some years in his father's timber yard where he was 'an example of sobriety and industry'. Yet in 1743, when he was 17, he became discouraged and 'formed the intention of going abroad, with a view to acquire wealth'. It is not clear what troubled him: difficult relations with his father, poor prospects for the business, or possibly a sense of the Mersey shore's remoteness from exciting events elsewhere.

Although the reference to a desire to 'acquire wealth' abroad suggests that William thought he was unlikely to find it in his father's firm or Liverpool, this is probably not the case. By the 1740s, Liverpool was a booming town, and firms like Rathbones were being swept along by a powerful current of business growth. However, speculation about William III's motives is academic since he obviously did stay on, and by 1746, the year his father died, the firm was calling itself William Rathbone & Son. As the new head of the business, the young William's desire to acquire wealth became the driver for a rapid expansion in many dimensions: new activities, new destinations and new commodities.

The first official indication we have of the existence of the Rathbones business is in 1766 when Liverpool's trade directory includes 'Rathbone, William, Timber Merchant, Duke Street'. This is a rather modest entry for a business which we know had by then expanded well beyond timber, but here may be an indication that timber was still the dominant activity, and that it was as a timber merchant that William III was best known. This was certainly the case in 1757, a year for which the firm's letter book survives. Correspondence shows William dealing in beech from the Baltic, mahogany from Jamaica and tall firs for masts from America. But his interests in shipping are widening: he is dashing off letters to ship captains and correspondents in Ireland, Holland, Danzig, Sweden, Norway, the West Indies, Boston, Philadelphia and many places besides, demonstrating a wide though, given Liverpool's expanding horizons, not untypical geographical spread. Mostly, this trade consisted of exporting local products such as salt, coal, earthenware and glassware, textiles and kelp in exchange for commodities such as sugar, tobacco, grains and more

William Rathbone III.

specialised goods such as tallow, iron and even butter.

We do not know whether William III actually owned the ships that transported these goods, or whether he hired them. Several advertisements in the *Liverpool Chronicle* and *Gazette* announcing sailings give Rathbones as the handlers, one of them mentioning 'good accommodation for passengers', showing a different side to the business, though this does not necessarily mean he was the owner.

The skilful management of ship movements to make the best use of hold space was key to the success of the business. In 1757 William III wrote to one of his agents asking that 'no room be left unfilled. If any goods offer on freight, you may accept the same if it be on such terms as will be to my advantage.' This need to fill ships to the brim helps explain why he diversified into so many different, often highly exotic, commodities. In February 1757 he wrote to his agents in Danzig, Corry & Elliott, to inform them that 'Carolina indigo sells here at 5/- to 8/- per pound as in quality. Rice may at present be shipt at 14/- to 16/- per Cd, which is rather higher than at present it is in London. Pymento is advanced both in London and here and

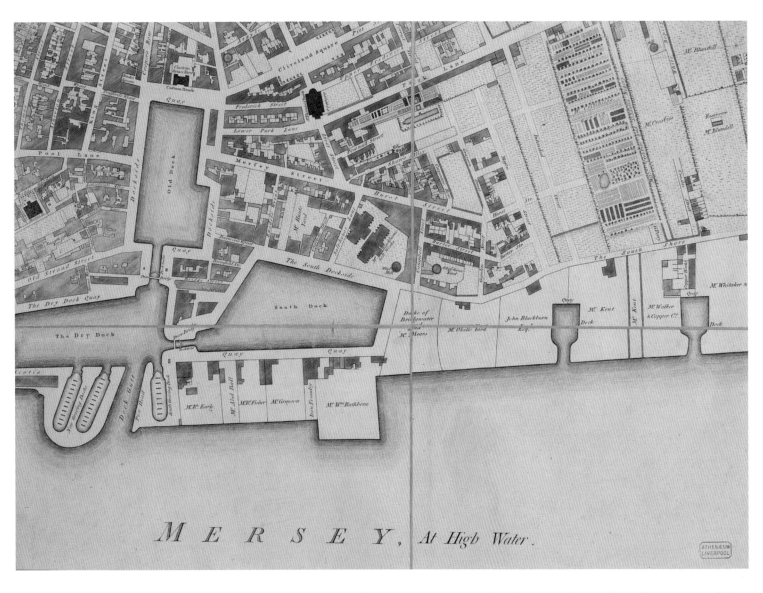

Plan of Liverpool by George Perry, 1769, showing the premises of 'Mr. Wm. Rathbone' on the waterfront.

must with all other West India commodities certainly be higher than at present, otherways the trade will not bear the high freights and insurance now going...'

Always on the look-out for new opportunities, William III made history for Liverpool by becoming, in 1784, the first merchant to import cotton from America rather than the West Indies, the main supplier until then. But the novel consignment caused a kerfuffle. Navigation laws required foreign imports to be carried by English ships or ships of the country of origin. Rathbones cotton arrived in an American ship. Since customs officials had not heard of American cotton, they assumed it was West Indian, therefore illegal, and seized it. The mistake was soon sorted out, but William's enterprise was not quickly

rewarded because the market also mistrusted this new commodity. The consignment was only sold with difficulty to a dealer in Derby. (This account, a favourite with the Rathbone family, has been contested by researchers who found evidence of earlier, smaller consignments of cotton. There is even confusion about the exact date. In any case, the story has acquired the force of legend.) The amount was very modest, a mere eight bags and three barrels, but it was the beginning of a massive trade for the emerging port: within 20 years Liverpool was handling nearly 200,000 bales a year. The expansion of American cotton followed the collapse of the West Indian business in the late 1700s with the rebellion of slaves on several plantation islands, notably the French colony of St Domingo in 1791–92.

25

Managing this increasingly complex business required William III to pay close attention to detail, and have considerable trust in the honesty and competence of his captains and agents. In 1758 he writes to one of his captains: 'Keep clear account, be as frugal as possible in thy expenses, and don't neglect writing by all opportunities with an account of thy proceedings.' Keeping a clear account was vital. Without banks or international currencies, merchants like William III had to rely on bills and letters of credit to clear their finances, or in extremis gold, though that was risky. The clearing centre for bills on European trade at the time was Amsterdam, and William's letters include instructions to his agents there to set up credits. Later, he changed his arrangements to make his payments through London, where he put up a bond of £1,000 with his bankers, which he believed to be adequate since he had 'seldom required more than £1,500 being guaranteed at one time'. One problem he faced was that since any transaction of more than £10 was settled

with bills, he was often short of hard cash to pay the firm's small expenses and wages.

He was also quick to protect his reputation with unsatisfied clients. An Irish timber merchant, William Greenhow, wrote to him on June 15th 1757 to complain about the quality of a shipment of mahogany which he had received from Rathbones' Dublin trader. William III wrote back:

Esteemed Friend,
…Am surprised at the character thou gives the mahogany sent thee per the Dublin Trader, it being quite the reverse of what it deserves. There's not one plank in the parcel but what's of the growth of the Island of Jamaica, and so far from being the refuse of a Cabinet Maker's yard that it was the best I could pick out of a large quantity in which I was neither deceived nor imposed upon as I have an account by me what ships brought all the Parcels I bought them from …. I can prove they are the growth of the North Side of the Island of

An armed merchant ship on the River Mersey, 1780. William Rathbone III insisted on filling all his ships to the brim, and wrote to an agent that 'no room be left unfilled. If any goods offer on freight, you may accept the same if it be on such terms as will be to my advantage.'

Working sketch for J.T. Serre's engraving, *Liverpool from the Cheshire Shore* (1798), shows a privateer on the right and a naval warship on the left. Shipping goods became a dangerous business with wars, privateers and pirates to contend with and William Rathbone III complained bitterly when insurance rates on the transatlantic routes rose to almost 'ruinous' amounts.

Manning the Navy – a press gang at work, 1790. War at sea unleashed press gangs on ports like London and Liverpool which forced sailors into the navy.

Jamaica where all the best mahogany comes from, and could likewise make it appear the very plantation they grew upon …. Am sorry this parcel hath not answered thy expectations, and if I had sent thee any rotton [*sic*] Mahogany from Jamaica should think myself in justice obliged to take the same to my own account…

William III frequently had to contend with one of the recurrent tribulations of merchanting – war – though, as Birrell put it: 'In the Liverpool of the 18th century, war was never unpopular.' War disrupted shipping and held up construction of the new docks. In May 1757 William III complained in a letter about the problems of getting his goods out of America, where European wars had their repercussions: 'Our principal dependence of wheat from abroad is from America but none is yet arrived, neither is it known here when we may expect any, as by the last accounts from here, an Embargo was laid on all ships in the English Provinces, which was not known how long might continue.' War also unleashed the scourge of press gangs which raided ports like Liverpool for naval manpower, adding to the risks merchantmen already faced from privateers and pirates. These risks drove insurance rates on the transatlantic routes to 10 guineas per £100, which William III described as 'almost or altogether ruinous to commerce'.

But war also brought benefits. Hostilities on the Continent and in the English Channel drove business away from south coast ports and Bristol towards the Irish Sea and into Liverpool's lap. Williamson's Liverpool Memorandum Book published in 1753 claimed that during war 'trade flourished and spread her wings' because Liverpool was 'a passage little known to the enemy … which invited numbers of strangers from different parts to begin trade and settle here'. War also disrupted markets and drove up prices, but this was all good if you knew what was going on and could speculate accordingly.

Moreover, war opened up new territories for business: There were fresh colonies and plantations, new sources and destinations for trade. Britain was almost permanently at war between 1739 and 1815,

Richard Gildart, aged 96, by Joseph Wright of Derby painted in 1768. Gildart, a leading Liverpool merchant of the 18th century, traded in commodities such as salt and sugar and owned ships that transported slaves. He served as mayor three times and was a Member of Parliament for 20 years.

yet this coincided with one of the golden ages of Rathbones' and Liverpool's fortunes.

That William III was an ambitious, even aggressive, businessman we can deduce from events in the next few years when he pushed hard to expand Rathbones' physical presence in Liverpool. In 1768 he took a lease on 'ground and dwelling house, four several warehouses and buildings thereon situated on West side of Salthouse Dock'. This was beside the new dock which had been completed in 1754. A map of Liverpool in 1796 outlines the sites of various businesses along the dock, and shows Rathbones to be much the largest, consisting of a timber yard, a warehouse and a counting house. This was where the Rathbones business was to be based for the next 60 years. But William III was still not satisfied. In 1776 he petitioned the corporation to allow him to enclose further land adjoining his site. Permission was refused, but he went ahead anyway, and added a causeway to connect it to his wharf. The corporation ordered him to remove the causeway because it was obstructing shipping, but allowed him to keep the land. Still unsatisfied, William III then extended his premises once more and encroached upon the neighbouring dock belonging to the Duke of Bridgewater, triggering a dispute which dragged on for several years.

But if this suggests that William III had high-handed tendencies, he was by then quite a grandee in Liverpool, a man of wealth and stature who played a prominent role in the town's affairs, a member of the mercantile elite. The 1783 Liverpool directory describes him simply as 'Merchant', a step up from 'Timber Merchant' in earlier directories, and a sure sign of attainment.

A recent history of Liverpool in the 18th century describes the town's mariner-merchants as 'the key social group', who 'bound together Liverpool society, linking politics, trade and finance to build a commercial community.' The merchants were also 'the catalysts for economic development, moving easily between different forms of money-making, investing in voyages, purchasing shares in industrial concerns and engaging in property speculation'. Day-to-day, their world revolved around the docks and wharves on the Mersey and the Exchange – or the 'Change as it was known – where they traded deals and gossip. In William III's time the 'Change was a relatively modest building, soon to be replaced

by a massive classical pile costing over £100,000, Liverpool's grandest construction thus far. Given their wide-ranging interests, these powerful businessmen were able to use their clout to benefit the town, for example by lobbying for acts of Parliament (needed to build the docks and license new trade routes), and obtaining credit from London financiers for their ambitious municipal projects. This group came to dominate local politics and the corporation. They also formed the core of the pro-slavery lobby as the abolition debate began to rage in the late 1700s: they were a tough lot who let little stand in their way.

Culturally, they probably lacked polish. Samuel Derrick, the Master of Ceremonies of elegant Bath, visited Liverpool in 1760 and observed that while their tables were 'plenteously furnished' with rum, 'few of the merchants have had more education than befits a counting house', though to be fair on the perceived philistinism of 18th-century Liverpool, the town did open a public library before London in 1758, funded by local philanthropists including William Rathbone.

These merchants nonetheless shared the pretensions of the fashion-conscious early Georgian age. Birrell gives us the following description of a successful Liverpudlian from around this time:

'In the latter half of the 18th century, a Liverpool merchant or banker wore, whilst going about his business, a Court dress coat, with a stand-up collar and gilt or silver buttons. His waistcoat was long, with majestic flaps, worthy of the snuff-box that lurked in one or other of its capacious pockets; his breeches were short and buckled at the knee. His stockings on a fine day would be silk, and in bad weather cotton or woollen. He had ruffles at his wrist, and a white stock supported his chin and gave dignity to his carriage. He could wear a cocked hat and flourish a gold- or ebony-headed cane. He had more wigs than one – tie wigs, bush wigs, brown wigs, and, if he wore his own hair, it was well powdered. Here was a gentleman indeed, well worth arrest, and comely to look upon! No wonder a favourite text with clerical candidates for Corporation preferment was the one which speaks of Tyre as "the crowning city whose merchants are princes, whose traffickers are the honourable of the earth".

'This "weel-put-on" gentleman dined in his own home in Castle Street or Water Street or Old Hall

Leading Liverpool merchants were members of the Ugly Club, founded in 1743. The club's rules said all members must have an ugly face and would be fined for lateness or consuming insufficient alcohol.

Street or Hanover Street at one o'clock, though, on a Saturday, when he dined with his club or at an Inn, dinner would be served as late as half-past two or even three o'clock. The Counting Houses were kept open till seven or even eight in the evening when, the leisurely toils of the day over, a good supper would send the honourable trafficker contented to his bed.'

The final paragraph may not be entirely accurate because Liverpool also sported male drinking and dining clubs which were typical of these increasingly flamboyant times. One was the Ugly Club, founded in 1743, whose rules specified that all members must have an ugly face and must pay fines if they were late or did not drink enough. For more general entertainments, there was a playhouse, built in the 1740s by Thomas Steers of wet dock fame. True to its love of big things, Liverpool then went on to build the most expensive provincial theatre in Britain, the Theatre Royal, which opened in Williamson Square in 1772, paid for by local investors and benefactors.

The reigning culture was one of conspicuous but well-earned wealth, and lax Protestantism (Catholicism came later with the inflow of Irish immigrants). Birrell recounts that it was customary for the mayor to attend church service on Sunday mornings and retire to the town hall for a hearty lunch with his 'cronies' which lasted until the assembled company was reminded that it was time to return for the evening service. As for the ordinary people, they customarily attended church only every other

Williamson Square by William Herdman. Liverpool merchants invested enthusiastically in the Theatre Royal, Williamson Square. It was financed by 30 shares of £200 which sold out within hours of being offered. The theatre opened in 1772 and was one of the largest and most prestigious provincial theatres in Britain.

Sunday 'without thinking any harm'.

But William III would not have approved. Although his portrait shows him to be well dressed and well fed, contemporary descriptions make him out to be a sober and devout man, true to his Quaker roots. A good friend, the Rev. Thomas Clarkson, said of him after his death: 'Though he lived in a state of pecuniary independence, he gave an example of great temperance, as well as great humility of mind.' William III would have nothing to do with Liverpool's flourishing trade in alcohol: rum from the West Indies and wine from southern Europe. Another young friend, Dr Rutter, wrote in 1835 that 'in business he was very diligent and active; yet the concerns of business disturbed him not: and when at the close of day he sat down with his family, there was such calmness, such composure in his aspect and demeanour that it was almost impossible for those who were near him not to feel the full influence of it'. Rutter recounted how, when he was still making his way as a young man, William III took him under his wing and told him: 'Now in this large and dangerous town, thou mayest probably often be invited into company which may be neither profitable nor agreeable to thee. In all such cases, thou hast a ready excuse. Thou art always engaged to me.' Rutter admits that he often availed himself of this offer.

One reason for William III's fatherly treatment of Rutter is that he, William, was married to Rachel Rutter, who was probably Rutter's aunt, and descended from Richard Rutter with whom his father, William II, had gone into business in 1730. Rachel bore him three children, two girls and a boy who was to become William IV. After Rachel died in 1761, William III married again, this time to Margaret Fletcher; altogether he had 11 children, eight of whom died young.

As a Quaker, William III took an active part in the affairs of his sect, becoming a preacher in which role he travelled widely, spreading the word. He also became a trustee of the Hackins Hey meeting house, and in 1766 was appointed to oversee alterations to the building, supplying timber for the repairs himself. His religious affiliation came through most strongly in his opposition to the slave trade at a time when 'blackbirding', as it was called, was the source of much of Liverpool's business and wealth. Whether William III was a lifelong opponent of slavery, as tradition would have it, or a late convert is not entirely clear. In 1768, when he was 42 years old, a letter shows that he bought a 14-year-old black boy called Tom for £31 10s and shipped him to Lübeck. The letter to his agent says: 'I have a good character of his disposition and honesty; his late master has always accustomed him to go with the other servants to worship, in which he is very regular, both public and in his own family.' He goes on to list Tom's clothing: '9 pairs of stockings, two shirts, a drab coat and waistcoat, a blue coat and waistcoat, one pair of leather breeches, one silk handkerchief, one silk cravat, one pocket handkerchief, one hat, one blue riding coat and a pair of shoes.' Including commission of half a per cent and shipping expenses, the total value of the transaction came to £32 12s 1d. It might not have been quite as odious as packing dozens of unclothed Africans off to America in shackles, but it was traffic in human beings nonetheless.

Temptation continued to dog his path. Nearly 20 years later (the exact date is uncertain, but given the circumstances it cannot have been before William IV's marriage in 1786), according to family recollections, his son William IV discovered that his father was in correspondence with a friend in Bristol who wanted him to take a share in a blackbirding venture. William IV told his wife that he intended to remonstrate with his father about this, but she urged him to be careful. 'For', she said, 'he will never get over his son's having made such a remonstrance, and how will you ever meet him in this world after it?' To which William IV replied: 'Yes, but how can I meet him in the next world if I don't?' The upshot was that William IV did remonstrate with his father; the old man saw that his son was right and gave the venture up. He did, apparently, feel the remonstrance very deeply, and this may have been the turning point because soon afterwards, in 1788, he became a founder member (with his son) of the Liverpool branch of the Society for the Abolition of the African Slave Trade. Among his contributions to the Society, he supplied muster rolls of slave ships which he obtained from the Liverpool Customs House. These showed the high mortality among sailors on slave ships and undermined the slave trade's argument that it provided 'a nursery for British seamen'.

By the time of his death in 1789, William III was well known for his staunchly anti-slavery views, so much so that any memory of his dealings in that business had been obliterated. The Rev. Clarkson, who became a leading abolitionist campaigner alongside William Wilberforce, noted in his obituary of his friend: 'However humble he appeared, he had always the courage to dare to do that which was right, however it might resist the customs or the prejudices of men. In his own line of trade, which was that of timber merchant on an extensive scale, he would not allow any article to be sold for the use of a slave ship, and he always refused those who applied to him for materials for such purpose.' Among William III's papers were found the drafts of two advertisements which he intended to publish in the Liverpool newspapers 'stating the ground of his refusal to furnish anything for this traffic upon Christian principles'.

The strain of running the demanding business that Rathbones had now become began to tell in later life. In 1784, when he was nearly 60, William III decided to step back and hand the reins to his son William IV, who was then 27 and had been involved for some years. William III wrote to his clients:

'We take this opportunity of informing thee that our W.R. Senr., having for some time wished to lessen the number of his commercial concerns, hath now concluded to retire from that part of our connection which consisted of the Commission business. The weight of this hath principally been conducted by our W.R. Junr. for some years, and the management of it is under his direction. It is therefore now concluded that this branch of our business shall in future be carried on by him for his own account.'

The announcement carries the implication that there was another branch of the business with which William III would continue to be connected, most likely one which did not require the tedium of day-to-day management, such as looking after the family's investments.

William III lived another five years. According to a detailed account of his final hours by his daughter Elizabeth, he had been exceptionally busy on Quaker business, including attending the Society of Friends' annual meeting in London. But he was then taken by an unnamed illness. On the evening of August 10th 1789, he lapsed into delirium, broken by moments of lucidity when he declaimed passages from the Bible. Early on the morning of the 11th, he asked to be taken to the next room where the air was fresher. He died around 9 am surrounded by his wife and children.

By the time of his death, Rathbones was firmly on the Liverpool map, one of the largest firms on Merseyside, now more a merchanting than a timber and shipbuilding business. History may have been kind to him so far as his anti-slavery record was concerned, but William III added further strength to the Rathbones' reputation for compassion and good works, and left his sons a strong inheritance.

The anti-slave trade campaign's emblem, designed by Josiah Wedgwood, depicted a kneeling slave, with the famous motto, 'Am I not a man and a brother?' Reproduced widely on pottery and medallions, the emblem soon became an icon for the abolitionist movement.

Liverpool and slavery

The slave trade was big business in 18th-century Liverpool; some have even described it as the 'mainspring of the city's wealth' – a stain on its history for which the city issued a formal apology in August 2000 and opened the International Slavery Museum in the Albert Dock in 2007.

Although the transatlantic slave trade dates back to the 16th century, an organised trade in captured Africans really began in the early 18th century, shortly before William Rathbone II arrived in Liverpool. The booming sugar plantations in the West Indies created an insatiable demand for labour, a commodity that the Merseyside merchants were keen to supply. The first link with Liverpool is found in 1700 in papers belonging to the Norris family, important merchants in the area. An unsigned letter instructs a captain to secure slaves from the Gold Coast and proceed as speedily as possible across the Atlantic to sell them to plantation owners in Barbados, where his ship would be loaded up with sugar and rum to finance the journey home, completing the infamous 'Golden Triangle', the route that was followed by most slavers.

A few years later, in 1709, Liverpool teamed up with other budding ports and manufacturing towns such as Bristol, Exeter and Birmingham to petition against the monopoly of African trade routes held by the Royal African Company. The monopoly was not lifted until 1750, but by then Liverpool's impatient slavers were already engaged in slave trading in a big way. In 1753 a local directory records the names of 101 Liverpool merchants involved in the trade, many of them the town's most respected burghers.

According to one estimate, Liverpool ships undertook some 5,000 slaving voyages between 1700 and 1807, when the slave trade was finally abolished. This equates to 48 a year, or nearly one a week, with each ship capable of carrying 250 slaves. In the year before abolition, 185 slave ships left Liverpool with capacity for nearly 50,000 slaves. One may wonder how the plantations managed to absorb such huge numbers; one reason was that it was 'cheaper to buy a slave than to breed one'.

The artist Henry Fuseli (1741–1825), who visited Liverpool around this time remarked: 'Methinks I everywhere smell the blood of slaves.' Liverpool was not itself a market for slaves, but one of the perks enjoyed by slaver captains was the right to choose the best slaves for themselves, and bring them home to keep as servants or sell.

It is important to realise that slave trading was a legal, licensed activity of which most

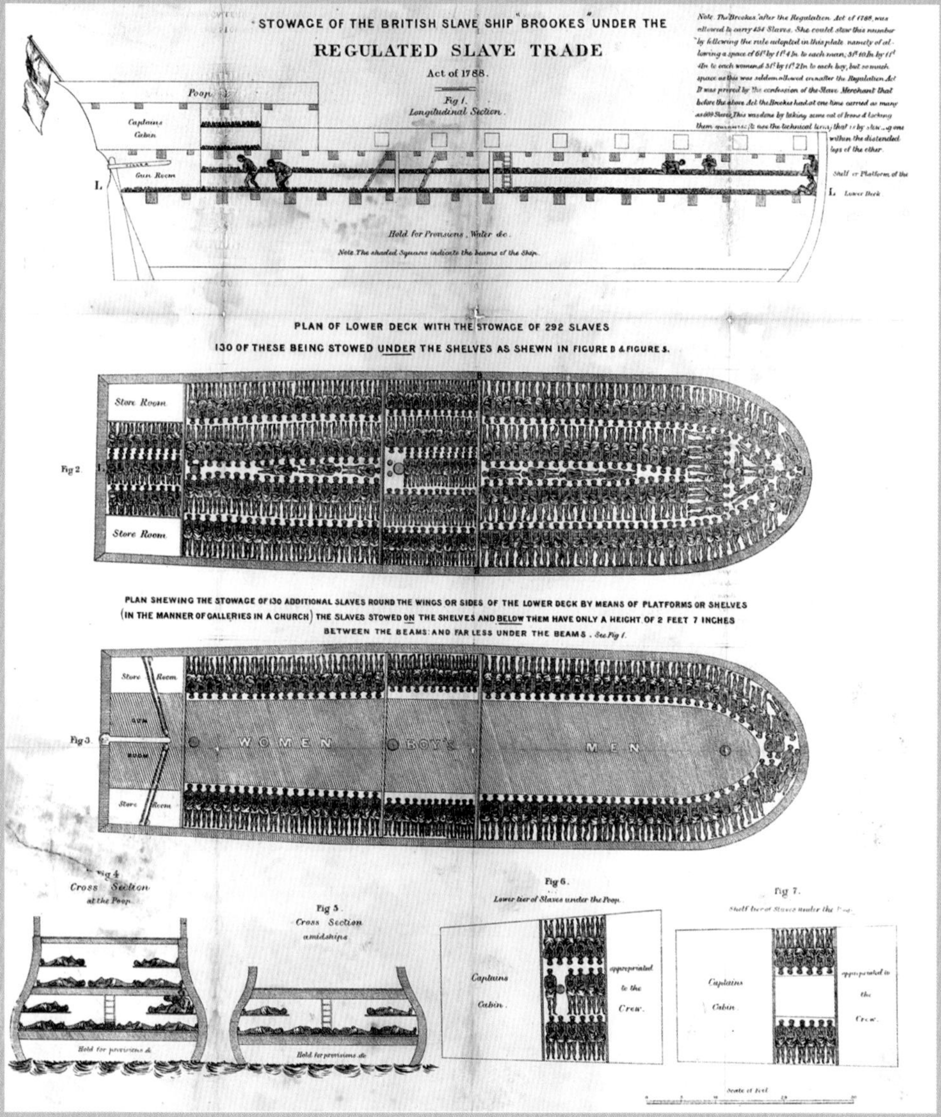

This illustration shows how slaves were stowed on board the British slave ship *Brookes* in 1788. The image was much used by abolitionists in their fight to end the trade. After the 1788 Regulation Act, *Brookes* was allowed to carry 454 slaves, the approximate number shown in this illustration. However, in earlier voyages she carried between 609 and 740 slaves.

Treating for Slaves, 1798 was printed by the anti-slavery movement. The inscription at the bottom of the print reads:
Fleecy looks and black complexion
Cannot forfeit Nature's claim
Skins may differ, but affection
Dwells in Black & White the same.

Liverpudlians were very proud. They saw it not only as supporting Britain's colonial expansion, but as adding to the legitimate prosperity of their town. Any suggestion that it was wrong would almost certainly have been greeted with hostility or incredulity. In 1788 a local newspaper carried the following item from a reader: 'In what light but in that of enemies of their country can we look upon those who, under the specious plea of establishing universal freedom, endeavour to strike at the root of this trade, the foundation of our commerce, the support of our colonies, the life of our navigation, the first cause of our national industry and riches?' It was often said on Merseyside that if the abolitionists succeeded, 'the grass would soon grow in the streets of the town'.

Even so, there were people in Liverpool who had misgivings about the trade, among them William III and William IV, but they had to tread carefully because vocal opposition would earn them enemies in a world built very much on personal relationships. Nonetheless, in 1788, the abolitionists felt bold enough to set up a local branch of the Society for the Abolition of the African Slave Trade. A measure of its popularity may be gauged from the fact that it initially attracted only 18 members, including Williams III and IV.

But as anti-slavery sentiment spread through Britain in the late 1700s, Liverpool gradually found itself driven from the position of national consensus to defensive minority, and eventually into the losing camp when Parliament voted to abolish slavery in Britain and its colonies in 1807.

Abolition had unexpected consequences, however. It put a stop to the trade in slaves, but not to the use of slaves in overseas plantations, which meant that Liverpool ships continued to trade profitably in the produce of slave labour, particularly cotton and sugar. But once the slave trade became illegal, public opinion in Liverpool swung sharply against it, and the town put itself at the forefront of the campaign to abolish slavery in the British colonies, which happened in 1833. The motive was not entirely philanthropic: it was also to prevent the French and Spanish, who had not abolished slavery, gaining an unfair trading advantage. Nor did the volume of Liverpool's shipping business diminish as its ships found new opportunities, for example in China's teas and silks. In fact, the abolition of slavery preceded one of the most prosperous eras in Liverpool's history.

Campaigner Thomas Clarkson addresses the Anti-Slavery
Convention, 1840, attended by more than 500 delegates,
including abolitionist Richard Rathbone, the son of William
Rathbone IV. Clarkson set up a mainly Quaker group whose
work led to the passing of the Abolition of the Slave Trade Act
by the British parliament in 1807. The Convention, attended by
figures such as the liberated slave Henry Beckford, called for
the worldwide abolition of slavery.

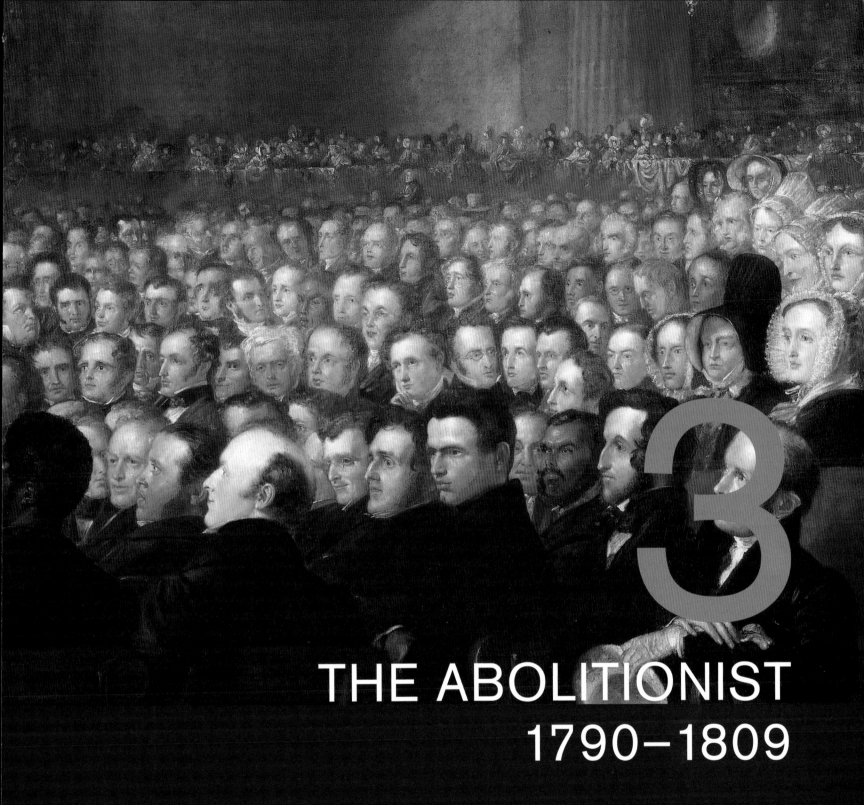

THE ABOLITIONIST
1790–1809

3

The fourth William is the first to put the Rathbone name on the public stage: a dynamic figure of high erudition, passionate about the great causes of the day, a fighter, a non-conformist almost to the point of recklessness. There was hardly an issue in late 18th-century Britain on which he was not a campaigner: slavery, war, social deprivation. He declaimed his views at meetings and public gatherings in Liverpool and London, and poured out his heart and mind in a stream of colourful letters, dozens of which have survived. He had, according to one biographer, 'a fierce determination to leave nothing unsaid'. No one could reproach him for the firmness of his beliefs, for his honesty and commitment, though whether he made much of a difference in his own time is open to question. Eleanor Rathbone, his great-granddaughter and herself a public figure as a 20th-century MP, described him as 'a man born to belong to minorities and to champion lost causes'. However, many of those causes did come right in the end, suggesting that a fairer description is a man in advance of his times.

The Iron Bridge at Coalbrookdale in Shropshire, 1780. William Rathbone IV married Hannah Mary Reynolds, who inherited shares in Coalbrookdale Iron Works on the death of her father. The Rathbone family were trustees and major shareholders in the bridge until 1950.

William Rathbone IV, painted by J. Allen.

If he differed from his calm and temperate father with his high public profile, he also contrasted with him in appearance. Unlike the burly, humourless figure of William III, the new William had a fine sensitive face, with wide questioning eyes, strong eyebrows and ruffled silver hair. An oil portrait done in later life by J. Allen catches him with an alert look, clutching a book, as if ready to launch into debate. The silver hair is itself indicative of the man: he was never in good health, and he died aged only 51, exhausted by his campaigns.

As the only son, he was reared to run the family business. Born in 1757, he left school at the age of 16 to join the family firm where he appears quickly to have learnt the ropes and taken on responsibility. Even at a young age he displayed the impetuous, romantic streak that shaped so much of his behaviour in later life. When 20, he fell in love with a young lady called Ann Younger, also a Quaker, who lived in Bishop Auckland. The two exchanged tender letters, and he, knowing that she collected 'curiosities', sent her some coral from the West Indies. Sadly, Ann died within a few months.

His erudition too was demonstrated at an early

41

stage. There is a charming letter to his sister Elizabeth, written in perfect copperplate when he was still very small, describing 'Mr Green's baloon [*sic*] … which went up from the poorhouse yard'. Even though he left school young, the apprentice William pursued his studies of history, economics, theology and philosophy in his spare time, sharpening his interest in the affairs of the world. He also taught himself French, Latin and Greek after work hours, usually kneeling on the floor with a wet towel wrapped around his head to aid concentration.

In 1786, nine years after Ann's death, William IV found a new love in Hannah Mary Reynolds, the daughter of Richard Reynolds, a wealthy Quaker philanthropist who had taken over the Coalbrookdale Ironworks after the death of Abraham Darby, his father-in-law. It was a wrench for Hannah to leave the family in Shropshire and live in Liverpool 70 miles away, but William III was insistent that his son and new wife set up their marital home on Merseyside and inherit the business.

We have already seen how William senior stepped aside in 1784 in favour of his son, who was by then widely recognised as the effective head of the family firm. When William III died in 1789,

Hannah Mary Rathbone.

William IV became at the age of 32 the owner of a substantial concern which included timber trading, passenger and cargo shipping, and the broad range of commodities typically handled by a Liverpool merchant. He quickly decided it was too much for one man and, lacking any male siblings, turned to his sister Sarah's husband, Robert Benson, who was a wholesale grocer in Kendal. The two formed a partnership called Rathbone & Benson. Family legend has it that the following year, 1790, a young stranger turned up in the office saying that he had heard up north that a Quaker firm had a large business in Liverpool, and since he was a Quaker too and preferred business to farming, could he be taken on? William IV was so struck by the lad's boldness that he hired him on the spot. It was a good choice; the young man was made a partner within three years.

The stranger's name was James Cropper, and he would grow into a leading Quaker figure and an outstanding member of the Liverpool business community, with many accomplishments to his name. Unfortunately for William, temporary complications in Cropper's personal life caused him to quit the firm very soon after he became a partner in 1795, and shortly afterwards Benson's health declined and obliged him to give up work as well. The Rathbone, Benson & Cropper partnership had to be dissolved in 1796, and William was left to cast around for new co-venturers. This was a great disappointment because William was probably not cut out to run a merchanting business, and did not enjoy it. He may even have reined it in to reduce the burden of managing it. He reveals in a letter in 1796 that, before the break-up, he had been planning to withdraw from the firm anyway and reduce his share of the profits because of his ever-present health problems and to spend more time with his family.

Family was important to him. By then he had three children, though one was soon to die of scarlet fever. His eldest son, the future William V, born in 1787, was also a sickly child and in 1788 William decided to lease a farmhouse outside the town to give him country air. This was Greenbank, which was to become the Rathbone family home for the next 150 years and acquire a rich history of its own. Initially, William and his family only used it in the summer, returning to their Cornhill home in the winter. Later, William bought it and turned it into a

In 1788, William Rathbone IV leased the estate and house of Greenbank from the Earl of Sefton to use as a country retreat. On William's death Greenbank was taken on by his widow, Hannah Mary. Greenbank was central to family life, and the Rathbones' association with the house was to last 150 years. Shown here is a sketch of the dining room by Mary Rathbone.

permanent residence.

Another reason for William's wanting to step back from the business must have been to indulge his passion for public causes. These ambitions had to be postponed because of the partnership problems, though he returned to them with fresh vigour once he had sorted the business out.

Though flamboyant, William IV was a cautious man, particularly when it came to business. There is much evidence of this. He once wrote to his son about the importance of putting part of the yearly profit into reserves, 'from the want of which much disappointment, suffering and embarrassment have frequently been occasioned'. He was also alert to the difficulties of forming successful partnerships which depended so much on personal relationships. Writing to his friend Dugald Bannatyne in Glasgow, to whom much of the surviving correspondence is addressed, he says: 'The delicacy & the importance of partnership connections are … such that too much caution could scarcely be used in forming them … in order to preserve that peace & independence which [they] too frequently unhappily destroy.' He goes on to lay out his requirements in partners.

'The qualifications most wanted are a competent knowledge of & experience in mercantile business, fair talents improved by education, quickness and facility in business (either in the purchase & sale of Goods, or the management of the correspondence, for each forms a distinct & an ample province for one person) & in an especial manner diligent persevering attention to business. Integrity is so essential where so much confidence would be bestowed that I need not dwell on it.'

The terms he offered to prospective partners were 'an immediate income of several hundreds a year, & in a few years it would probably exceed a thousand'. If the new partner could put capital into the business 'it would be an additional recommendation, but we are not disposed to make it an essential condition'.

Although William IV hoped that Bannatyne would find suitable candidates in Scotland because 'the education and habits of your Countrymen are in general extreamly [sic] favourable to business', he eventually settled on two young Liverpool brokers who were introduced to him by Benson. Their names were William Hughes and William McMurdo

Duncan, and he formed an initial three-year partnership with them called Rathbone, Hughes & Duncan. The articles of partnership say that William will provide the cornerstone to their venture by putting up £10,000 in capital on which he will be paid five per cent a year, while the other two 'will devote the whole of their time and attention to the conduct of management of the business'. William was to get 10/24ths of the profits, and the others 7/24ths each. This arrangement allowed William IV to shift management onto younger shoulders while still taking a good income, and free himself up for his other interests. So he must have been pleased.

William IV seems to have made the better choice in Duncan, who was the tough-minded son of a Scottish Unitarian minister, than in Hughes who was described as a man of 'considerable ability and energy, but inordinate ambition'. Hughes would sometimes get ahead of himself, and was once found by William, returning after a long illness, holding an imprudently large stock of cotton which he was financing at a high rate of interest. William ordered the stock to be sold, but Hughes dragged his feet and William was forced to bring in other merchants to get rid of it. This was not the only instance of trouble with Hughes. William later wrote to Duncan: 'You tell me that Mr Hughes is under the impression that for some time past I have felt a general dissatisfaction with the conduct of the office .... I need to inform you that I have always cherished an anxious desire that [the firm's] character for good faith, courtesy of manners and liberality of conduct should deserve to stand in the foremost class ... this has not been the case in several recent incidences.' Despite these strains, which bore out William's earlier concerns about Hughes, the partnership endured until his death in 1809.

The heart of the Rathbones business had now shifted away from timber and shipbuilding to merchanting and consignment, two activities that appeared similar – they both involved shipping goods – but entailed different degrees of risk and profitability. Merchanting, the more traditional of the two, was classic 'own account' trading in which the merchant bought goods hoping to sell them at a profit: the risk was entirely his. Consignment, a later development, was where a merchant accepted a cargo of goods and undertook to sell them on behalf of the owner for a commission. This was less risky, but also less profitable since commissions were set by competition and would typically be one to two per cent. The best trade was a consignment with a ready buyer at an agreed price, the worst was being left with speculative goods which could only be shifted at a loss. The skill of a Liverpool merchant lay in striking a balance between the two forms of trading, taking on the right amount of risk to deliver the desired level of profit.

William III, as we have seen, was very much in the merchanting business, trading his rice and indigo. His more cautious son steered Rathbones in the consignment direction, establishing a more conservative policy which was taken up by his descendants. But this was not just his nature: it was a reflection of the times. Trade was becoming more organised and competitive, and consignment was better suited to emerging patterns.

The consignment business was not an easier option: it also took skill and market knowledge. The merchant had to be able to convince the shipper that he knew markets and prices in order to win the consignment in the first place. Like his father, William IV dealt in a bewildering array of goods – manufactures, perishables, textiles, metals – though on the bustling Liverpool waterfront, this was not unusual. We may wonder today how William IV knew the price of 'mess pork in barrels' without a telephone or a Reuter screen, but there would have been half a dozen other dealers in that commodity with whom he could trade. He also built up networks of correspondents in foreign ports to provide market intelligence.

William IV took a special interest in the firm's trade with America, which had got over the break caused by the War of Independence (1775–1783), and was fast becoming the mainstay of the business, particularly cotton. He describes it in a letter: 'It is very safe (for we decline having any debts in America) as well as a respectable and productive business, but it requires a great deal of constant & diligent attention, & has regularly increased both in extent

The sale room at East India House, Leadenhall, London, 1808. The East India Company was one of the most powerful commercial organisations that the world had seen. In its heyday it had a monopoly on British trade with India and the Far East. William Rathbone IV campaigned against the monopolies, but it was not until 1813 that the East India Company's monopoly on trade with India was removed and it took another 20 years to overturn the monopoly on trade with China.

and profits, though for some years we have rather wished to keep it within its former limits.' One of his young apprentices, Thomas Thornely, later told William VI, William IV's grandson, that Rathbones might have as many as 25 ship consignments in the dock at any one time. In addition, William IV was running passenger services to the main American and Canadian ports. In 1801 William IV and Duncan were among the founders of the Liverpool American Chamber of Commerce, which was to exist for over 100 years and have many Rathbone family members and associates among its officers.

It was partly to protect his overseas trade that William IV threw himself into political lobbying and thence more widely into public affairs. An early issue for him was the monopoly enjoyed by the East India Company over trade with Britain's growing possessions around the African Cape and further east. In the 1770s, Liverpool merchants were among those agitating for an end to this privilege, but their efforts were thwarted by the French Revolution in 1789. William IV took up the cudgels again in 1792, drafting a call for action which he advertised in 23 newspapers and all the main ports. He also helped organise a public meeting in Liverpool which passed a resolution urging reform of the Company, but this was ignored by the government. He was back at it in 1807 to oppose a bill to raise the borrowing power of the Company. But this turned into one of his many lost causes, not least because Liverpool itself was divided on the issue – some merchants benefited from the monopoly. William complains in a letter about 'the supineness of the merchants of Liverpool' and the fact that they prefer 'wine and a good dinner' to political agitation. It was not until 1833, more than 20 years after his death, that the monopoly was finally abolished.

Although the campaign against the East India Company was motivated by his business interests, it also fitted William's wider concern for justice and fairness, always tempered by a strong belief in the virtue of commerce which he saw as 'one of the main sources of the prosperity and dignity of England, and as a mighty instrument of civilisation'.

William IV was particularly fascinated by the revolutions in America and France which so strongly coloured the political background to his life. He welcomed both these huge events as presaging an end to tyranny, and opening up a new age of human liberties based on the writings of philosophers and economists such as Thomas Paine, David Hume and Thomas Robert Malthus, all of whom he had devoured in his studies. He wrote that the revolutions 'will serve as experiments how far our theories are reducible to practice in the reform of old governments, for with respect to new, the whole business is done in America, and so much has had a pretty fair trial in France'. As this comment, made in 1793, suggests, he was optimistic about America, but less so about France where King Louis XVI had just been guillotined and the Reign of Terror was setting in. William goes on to deplore the French people's 'want of magnanimity' in their treatment of their king. He was soon to become very disillusioned by the outcome of the French Revolution, and began to worry about the possibility of war between Britain and France.

With clouds gathering, William launched a vigorous campaign against war and the person he saw to be its main agent, Prime Minister William Pitt the Younger. This was partly out of concern for his business, but also because he despised war as cruel and wasteful. His letters are littered with tirades against Pitt, whom he describes as 'an evil genius', and against his country's 'warlike character'. Even his own friends, he complains, 'drink to Pitt and war most cordially'. In 1795 he managed to get together a petition to King George III with 4,000 signatures calling for an end to war, but again, to no avail. His hopes were raised a few years later when Napoleon came to power with promises to stop wars. William IV was deeply impressed by Napoleon who, he believed, 'sincerely desires peace', though here too he was to be disappointed.

His particular anxiety was that war in Europe would spill over into America where Britain and France had large competing interests, and damage his nation's trade. He wrote of his fear that 'in falling out with France and America, we shall surely fall too'. These were prescient words because, in 1805, Napoleon issued a decree blockading British ports and ordering the seizure of British goods and subjects found on the high seas. This provoked retaliatory orders by Britain, which in 1806 imposed similar measures on French ports and property, but with the additional stricture that the measures should apply to neutral ships trading with the French. Intentionally or not, this struck at the heart

The end of the 18th century was a period of political tumult with revolutions in France and America. William Rathbone IV was a fierce opponent of war and had high hopes in 1804 when Napoleon came to power that peace would prevail. His hopes were soon to be dashed. This engraving shows Napoleon, surrounded by people of various faiths, advocating freedom of worship for all.

William Rathbone IV's book led to him being censured by his Quaker brethren.

ade, William IV went down to the House of Lords to testify. So eloquently did he speak that an account of the proceedings noted that 'a pin might have been heard to drop'. But his eloquence came to nothing. The ships of the British Navy seized and searched American merchantmen, provoking tensions with Washington and retaliation by President Thomas Jefferson. This confrontation, initially no more than a sidebar to the Napoleonic Wars, eventually led to Britain's invasion of America in 1812, with further devastating consequences for trade. It was only at that point that the orders were lifted, but, as with the East India Company campaign, William did not live to see the success of his cause.

Born and bred a Quaker, William IV took an earnest interest in religious affairs and the condition of his fellow men. He followed his father to become a trustee of the meeting house and helped to build a new one in 1791. But his passionate nature and restless mind made him an awkward member of the Society of Friends. He began to chafe against the orthodoxy of his fellow Quakers. In a letter to a friend in 1795 he wrote: 'I think much harm has been done to the cause of Christianity from representing its evidences as of so strong and imposing a nature as to be absolutely irresistible.' As Eleanor Rathbone said of him: 'He was too essentially a fighter to be at home in the Society of Friends.'

In 1804 William became interested in a recent incident in Ireland where a number of Friends had been 'disowned' for what were held to be 'lax views on the authority of the Bible' and for marrying outside the sect. The matter of marriage was a serious breach of Quaker discipline, which required not merely the offenders but also all family and friends who had attended the wedding to be ejected. This seemed to William to epitomise the tyranny of authoritarian Quakerism, and he decided to write an account of it to support his case. The book was published under the neutral-sounding title of *A Narrative of Events that have lately taken place in Ireland among the Society called Quakers*. It was the story of an incident rather than a polemic. But the book provoked a sharp reaction from his Quaker brethren, and in 1805 he was 'disunited' from membership of the Society for his lack of 'reverent regard for the whole of the Holy Scriptures'.

Through these actions, William broke the tradition of Quakerism in his own family and that of his

of American shipping which traded equally with Britain and France, and plunged the transatlantic trade into crisis. William was devastated and drummed up a campaign to have the orders lifted. 'If we let the present ministers go on,' he wrote, 'we are on the road to certain & speedy ruin.' A public meeting was held in Liverpool in 1808 at which he was one of the principal speakers. William dramatically outlined the scale of the threat to the town: ships from America made nearly 500 voyages to Liverpool every year, amounting to 123,000 tons. The value of this trade came to £20m a year and 'there is scarcely an individual in the place that is not affected by it, directly or indirectly'.

As leader of Liverpool's opposition to the block-

The Quakers

The Quaker faith played an influential part in the early history of Rathbones, inspiring the family with a strong sense of social duty, and sealing close business and family ties which all proved very fruitful.

The Society of Friends was formed in 17th-century England by a group of non-conformists led by George Fox, and it had immediate appeal as an alternative to the oppressive religious ideologies of the age, offering a direct and personal experience of God. It spoke particularly to plain folk, among them William Rathbone I, the yeoman of Gawsworth who became a convert around 1700 and was buried in the Friends Burial Ground in Macclesfield.

His son William II became a Quaker around 1731, shortly after he arrived in Liverpool, possibly under the influence of his father, but also because his second wife was a Quaker and, as such, could not marry a non-Quaker. Richard Rutter, his new partner, belonged to a staunchly Quaker family. The connection was reinforced by a series of marriages between Rathbones and Rutters and other Quaker families such as the Darbys, the Bensons and the Reynolds.

Quakers were noted for their industry, and good business sense. But the strict non-conformism of Quakers also marginalised them from mainstream society – though this was possibly less true in Liverpool which had a

strong tradition of dissent and was home to many religious causes. However, the feeling of being special strengthened the sense of community among Friends, and encouraged strong social and business networks. The early Rathbones went on long and frequent journeys around Britain and Ireland, meeting other Friends and helping to widen the community.

Many of the Rathbones' closest business connections were with other Quakers: they trusted each other, they employed each other, and helped each other out. James Cropper, the young man who walked in through William IV's door in 1790, was to become one of the leading Quaker businessmen of the age, leading ambitious ventures such as the building of the Liverpool & Manchester Railway, and going on to amass considerable riches as an overseas merchant.

But 19th-century Quakerism also had its tougher side: it imposed strict rules and had little tolerance of disobedience. William IV found this very irksome and was eventually expelled in 1804 for writing a tract critical of the Quakers' handling of dissent in Ireland. His son William V was also expelled for marrying outside the faith in 1812. Although this ended the direct connection between the Rathbones and the Quakers, the family tradition of public duty, good works and industriousness continued.

A Quaker meeting, 1735.

included Dr James Currie, a biographer of Robert Burns, the blind poet Edward Rushton, and from outside Liverpool Josiah Wedgwood of pottery fame, and John Dalton, the chemist, both of whom were personal friends of William's and at the forefront of innovation and enterprise.

A sense of what was driving William's espousal of reform can be drawn from this comment to a friend: 'I confess I cannot well conceive a more degrading spectacle than the prospect this country now exhibits. The opulence of the rich and the wretchedness of the poor ... and the disavowal of all the legitimate principles of government.' Liverpudlians had been stung in June 1780 by a comment from the American loyalist, Samuel Curwen, about Liverpool's condition: 'Houses by a great majority in middling style, few rising above that mark; streets long, narrow, crooked and dirty in an eminent degree ... the whole complexion nautical and infinitely below our expectations.' The comment was specially telling since Curwen had left America to escape persecution for his loyalty to Britain.

The Friends campaigned on a wide range of issues, from relief for the poor and electoral reform to education and slavery, by organising petitions, holding public meetings and publishing tracts. They funded many of their activities themselves: William bought land to house the poor, Roscoe donated the

wife, but he was in no doubt that he had done the right thing. In a letter to a friend shortly afterwards he described his expulsion as 'a release from restraints to which my respect and regard for the Society induced me to submit', adding ominously: 'I may publish a few details of the manner in which the proceedings of my case have been conducted.' He never got round to it, and may even have tried to mend fences because he was buried in the Quaker burial ground when he died four years later.

William's concern for humankind and what he saw as the degradation of his country led him to take up many political campaigns for social reform. He helped found a group called the Friends of Freedom to lead the reform movement in Liverpool, which attracted a small though impressive following. Its leader was William Roscoe, a man of conspicuous talents who was born the son of a kitchen gardener and rose to become one of Liverpool's leading literary figures, as well as a lawyer, MP and banker. His literary reputation was built on learned biographies of medieval Italians for which he earned comparison with the great 18th-century historian Edward Gibbon. Other members of the group

royalties from his poem *The Wrongs of Africa*. One of William's particular concerns was the working conditions of the labouring classes. 'Do you not think', he asked a correspondent showing an early interest in a cause that was only later to catch on, 'that our manufacturers, & especially by the increasing subdivision of labor, are tending rapidly to degrade the character of those employed in them into ignorant machines & sensual brutes?'

With so many literary men involved, the Friends also encouraged Liverpool's cultural aspirations, which were budding thanks to growing wealth and a new fashion to do something 'outside trade'. The Friends even found a label: Liverpool was to become 'the Florence of the North'. These stirrings might seem incongruous in early 19th-century Liverpool, but they gathered pace over succeeding decades, eventually leading to the creation of many of the town's finest buildings, including the Town Hall and Exchange remodelled by James Wyatt, and St George's Hall. Roscoe even developed the concept of a 'merchant-scholar', a person of matching business and intellectual accomplishments who would draw together all that was finest in Liverpool.

But while talk of high culture was flattering to Liverpool's elite, most of the issues espoused by the Friends made them deeply unpopular with the rest of the merchant classes whose main interest lay in protecting their wealth and privilege. William IV came to be known on the 'Change as 'the hoary traitor' because of his white hair, and it is recounted that when a doctor called to treat his illness, he asked to arrive after nightfall so that he should not be seen. William was philosophical. He said in a letter: 'I know with my views on many subjects it is impossible I should be long clear of [unpopularity], and as I have thus expected it, I have nothing to suffer from disappointment.'

No issue engaged the Friends more deeply, or made them more unpopular, than slavery. Unlike his father, William IV was a dedicated abolitionist from an early age, having seen the slave ships and the wealth that accrued from them. He was particularly troubled by Britain's grand declarations of liberty and dignity while at the same time conducting a shameful trade in human beings. He pointed to 'the absurd boast of our freedom whilst we basely associate to enslave others, the tyranny... of our connection with Asia and the unexampled cruelty and

aggression of our commerce with Africa'. For once, this was to be an issue that caught the tide of national opinion. Away from the focused interests of ports like Liverpool, the public mood was gradually turning against the slave trade, and in Parliament the political momentum for abolition was building.

In 1806, a most astonishing event occurred in Liverpool. In the general election that year, William Roscoe stood for Parliament and, despite being long associated with the abolitionist cause and sharing William's unpopularity, was elected the senior member for Liverpool, the country's largest slaving port. His triumph had much to do with the fact that he was, by then, a towering literary figure with an imposing physical presence, and a man of humble origins made extremely good. It was a marvellous moment for William's and Roscoe's supporters, who celebrated with a magnificent dinner. At the end of the room stood a fine bust of Roscoe inscribed with the words: 'An honest man is the noblest work of God'. Roscoe took his seat in the House of Commons and spoke in favour of the Abolition Bill which went through in 1807. But only two months later Parliament was dissolved, Liverpool recovered its senses and voted Roscoe out. However, it was enough. For once, William IV was on the winning side.

Quite how he managed to devote so much time to good causes, let alone conduct such a voluminous correspondence, while also managing a flourishing business is a matter of wonder. One reason must be that Duncan and Hughes, despite the latter's faults, were good at running the firm day-to-day, but another is that he really was a man of exceptional energy who kept a close eye on the business even while pressing his campaigns. It is striking, for example, that his first reaction to the passage of the Abolition Bill for which he had fought all his life, was to consider the market opportunities. Within days he wrote to a friend: 'If the African trade is abolished so very hastily, it will be evident that many ships, much capital and much talent will be out of employ. Is this not a strong proximate cause for renewing and urging our application about opening up the East India trade?' We can be certain that the Rathbones business really did flourish under his leadership because he died in 1809 a wealthy man with an estate worth over £100,000 in the money of the day.

William Roscoe (1753–1831), historian, poet, art collector, lawyer, politician and philanthropist, rose from humble beginnings to become one of Liverpool's most influential citizens. In this painting by Sir Martin Archer Shee, Roscoe is shown as a scholar surrounded by books and on the table stands a bust of Charles James Fox, his political hero. He founded the Liverpool branch of the Anti-Slavery Society, helped to establish the African Institute and campaigned in Parliament to ban the slave trade, despite violent protests against him.

William IV lived for another two years after abolition, but in poor health and great pain – a stomach complaint that could not be diagnosed. Shortly before his death, he mused on the emptiness of worldly things, but suddenly exclaimed with a return of his old energy: 'But I love the world and should have wished to stay longer in it.' Before he died, he had the satisfaction of seeing both his sons, the future William V and his younger brother Richard, go up to Oxford where they received the education he never had.

One cannot leave the story of William IV without feelings of admiration for a man who poured so much energy into high causes, and also sympathy for the frustration he must have felt when so few of them succeeded. Eleanor Rathbone confesses to being struck 'by the contrast between the smallness of his achievement and the great impression which his character and abilities seem to have made upon them'. Roscoe's son and biographer, who knew him well, says that William IV was made of the same clay that moulded heroes and martyrs in former times, but 'being confined to private station expended his strength in contests the recollection of which has already passed away'.

Liverpool Town Hall, remodelled by James Wyatt after a fire in 1795 destroyed much of the building.

4

DUTY BEFORE BUSINESS
1809–1840

Was the family firm, now nearly 100 years old, up to the challenge?

Not really. William IV's death in 1809 left a gaping hole in the family. His two sons William V and Richard were still at Oxford, and there were no brothers or uncles to take on the business. Although the firm itself was still profitable, William IV's obsession with outside matters had shorn it of direction and left it struggling. As time went by, there were other complications too. Once his sons took over the business, they turned out to have less of their father's great energy and ambition. They shared his conscientious spirit, but William lacked his charisma, and Richard his dynamism. This was to have severe consequences for the fortunes of the firm.

William IV had nonetheless taken great care to prepare his sons for a life of business and public service. As boys they were tutored by the Rev. Theophilus Houlbrooke, a member of the Unitarian Church to which William IV had turned after his expulsion from the Quakers, although the two boys remained Quaker. They were then sent to a school in Hackney in London run by Thomas Belsham, a well-known non-conformist who had come to William IV's notice through his vocal support for the abolitionist cause.

William IV cared deeply for the well-being of his sons. While they were studying at Hackney he wrote to them that there was only one way to achieve happiness, and that was 'by adding to faith virtue, and to virtue knowledge'. He also slipped in a bank note for £30 'to be ready for your Christmas bills'. A constant sufferer himself, he frequently admonished his sons to look after their health. 'Be assured my dear William, that thou hast not yet attained in knowledge to the right appreciation of the value of health. In this respect thy father has long and grievously failed, and, as thou knowest, he has grievously suffered for it.' Not that it made much difference. Both his sons were also plagued by ill health. Like his father, William V suffered from persistent stomach problems which sapped his energy and 'made him often very undecided and depressed at home', according to a later account by his own son.

William IV shaped his heirs with what today we would call work experience. In 1805, when he was 18, William V was sent to the Rathbones counting house as an apprentice, joined shortly afterwards by Richard, and later moved on to work for Mr Maury, an American merchant and the US consul in Liverpool. William IV also made financial arrangements to advance his eldest son's career. When William V reached his majority in June 1808, William IV put £5,000 into Rathbone, Hughes & Duncan on his behalf with the wish that it would 'prove useful as capital when there may be a suitable opening for thy entering into business'.

What William IV did not prepare his sons for was the crisis in the partnership that his death was to cause. The survivors, Hughes and Duncan, refused to admit the boys to their new firm as partners, and insisted that they complete an apprenticeship. (The old partnership dissolved automatically on William IV's death, and Hughes and Duncan formed a new one.) Moreover, they declared their intention to retain the old firm's name with Rathbone in it, as well as the counting house and timber yard at Cornhill. Strictly, Hughes and Duncan were within their rights as surviving partners, but these conditions were unacceptable to the family and led to a damaging rupture, made worse by the fact that

Statue of William Rathbone V in Sefton Park, Liverpool.

Richard Rathbone, merchant in partnership with his brother, William Rathbone V, both were opponents of slavery.

Paradise Street Unitarian Chapel, 1829. The Rathbones became Unitarians after William Rathbone V married a Unitarian and was expelled from the Quakers as a result.

the family still lived for much of the time at the Cornhill house (William VI was born there in 1819).

William V and Richard were forced to set up a new firm of their own using inherited capital, and hope that their father's goodwill would follow them. They circulated a letter to their contacts announcing the formation of William & Richard Rathbone & Co. with the promise that 'a constant attention to the interest of our friends will form our only claim to the continuance of that confidence which our late Father so liberally enjoyed'.

Would the clients switch? Fortunately, their father's old partner James Cropper came to the rescue. Cropper was now a successful merchant in partnership with Robert Benson, and he remembered the kindness done to him by William IV. He

generously seconded his managing clerk, John Mure, to the new firm and circulated letters of recommendation to his correspondents in America. When the first ship sailed in from America, there was a moment of suspense as to who would get its goods, the old firm or the new. A fellow apprentice of Richard's in the Maury business called Alexander Maxwell happened to be strolling along the quay when it tied up. He asked the captain who the shipment was consigned to. 'To William and Richard Rathbone', came the reply. Most of Cropper's American correspondents chose to work with the new firm, and seven years later Hughes & Duncan ceased trading.

William V and Richard began very cautiously. They were only 21 and 22 years old, with virtually

57

no knowledge of business other than at a basic level. Only their work experience and father's teaching, increasingly out of date, guided them, and it was 'a very hard struggle'. They were not helped by the outbreak of war with America in 1812, which had been caused by the infamous blockade. Britain's invasion of America was the exception to the famous rule that war always benefited Liverpool: transatlantic trade slumped. Two thousand fewer American ships called at Liverpool in 1812 than in 1810, ruining many Merseyside merchants.

The brothers were choosy about the bills they accepted, and never granted credit of more than 60 days. They were not unjustified in their caution. Businesses and banks came and went with alarming speed, not least Clarke & Roscoe, a bank in which their father's friend William Roscoe was a partner. The bank ran into difficulty in 1816 and, despite Roscoe's gallant attempts to save it, folded in 1820. Roscoe was forced to sell off many of his possessions, including his precious library. This was painful for the Rathbone brothers because of their family's long association with Roscoe. But they refused to finance a rescue. When Roscoe had become a partner in the bank some years before, their father William IV noted that it 'possessed great property & doth immense business, but it certainly wanted more talents and firmness in those at the head of it'. This had prompted William V to remove the accounts of his younger brothers Theodore and Benson, though curiously he left other family accounts at the bank. The Rathbones were criticised for these actions, even though they suffered losses when the bank collapsed. However some years later, in 1857, the Liverpool Borough Bank of which William V was chairman also collapsed through overtrading in bills. The bank was wound up in an orderly fashion, though it must have dented the Rathbone finances: William V had lent it money and bought shares in it only a few months before. Fortunately, the firm's reputation was unaffected.

This aversion to risk meant that the brothers prospered less than their neighbours, though probably suffered fewer anxieties. According to William V's son, this led to the curious situation whereby the Rathbones were assumed by the rest of the Liverpool business community to be much better off than they really were. In fact, he says, his mother had to practise 'the very closest economy, for during the most active portion of my father's life, his means were very limited'. William V claimed not to want great riches. Early in his marriage he wrote to his wife, 'I have no desire for wealth for its luxury or for its own sake; I believe a very little addition to my present expense would satisfy every wish I have, and without those things that I wish, I feel that many, many blessings are my lot.'

The Rathbones business was still located at Cornhill on the waterfront. One visitor around this time was John James Audubon, the American ornithologist and painter who called on Richard in July 1826,

Self-portrait drawn by American painter and ornithologist John James Audubon during his stay at Greenbank in 1826.

The American Wild Turkey Cock, by Audubon.

Red-shouldered Hawk attacking Bobwhite Partridges, by Audubon.

Hodgson was an energetic young man who embarked on the first of many foreign missions by members of Rathbones to expand the business, a trend indicative of the age. With improved communications and new markets, firms like Rathbones needed to sharpen their contacts and business intelligence. In 1819 Hodgson set off to North America on a tour which lasted 16 months and took him to many of Rathbones' correspondents around North America and Canada, as well as visits to Indian tribes, Quaker settlements and even Monticello where he met Thomas Jefferson. But though he learnt a lot about America, he found it difficult to form a clear-cut picture. In a letter to Rathbones from Boston towards the end of his trip, he said of the prospects for cotton: 'I am much at a loss. Sometimes I get rather sanguine, disposed to do foolish things, at other times every avenue seems to close, and the future looks rather blue.' In particular Hodgson found that Rathbones' conservative view on credit was out of kilter with the liberal terms which were available on the local market. Hodgson felt unable to recommend that Rathbones loosen up, and returned home empty-handed. Shortly afterwards he left the firm to run the newly founded Bank of Liverpool. At that point, in 1824, the firm gave itself the name Rathbone Bros. & Co., and so it remained until the mid-1990s when it became Rathbone Investment Management Limited.

Although the Hodgson mission showed a new spirit of adventurousness, it didn't actually change the way the firm did business, and shortly after his departure, Rathbones entered a period of severe decline due to poor management. Trade volumes fell off and profitability shrank, so much so that Rathbones' standing as both firm and family in the Liverpool community was threatened. Part of the blame must lie with William V who became averse to the cotton business, which he characterised as volatile and speculative. He was right for a while: cotton slumped to its lowest level in 1837 due to overproduction, though it later picked up strongly. In the 1820s he also began to involve himself more deeply in public affairs and had less time to devote to the business. Since Richard was not willing to take initiatives in his place, the firm drifted – and missed out on the huge expansion in Liverpool's trade with America in the recovery that followed the 1812 war. William VI later said that 'the firm was

and described the scene: 'A full dozen clerks were at their separate desks, work was going on apace, letters were being thrown into an immense bag belonging to a packet that sailed this day [to America].' The heart of the business continued to be the cotton trade with America, but this was becoming more specialised and competitive with brokers and exchanges playing a growing role. This naturally put pressure on commission merchants like Rathbones who dealt in complete consignments. The firm clearly needed more manpower, and when John Mure retired from Rathbones in 1814 the brothers took in a new partner called Adam Hodgson, a fellow Quaker. The firm was renamed Rathbone, Hodgson & Co.

An engraving of Liverpool from across the River Mersey by William Daniell, 1815.

unprepared to make the necessary changes in their mode of conducting business or to undertake the new forms of business which the expansion in trade required... Although at the beginning of the period they were one of the principal houses in the American trade, during it their business seriously fell off.'

Like his father, William V pursued two completely different lives, one with the firm and one on the public stage, but the second increasingly came to dominate. The range of his interests also mirrored those of his father: religion, electoral reform, the condition of the poor. Despite his father's clash with the Society of Friends, William V was brought up a Quaker and had many Quaker business colleagues. But he shared his father's problems with Quaker discipline. In 1812 he married Elizabeth Greg, the daughter of a prosperous Manchester mill-owner. Elizabeth was a Unitarian, which meant that

William V had breached Quaker rules on marriage; as a consequence of this he too was expelled from the Society. There is a story that he was later re-admitted upon giving an assurance that, though he could not, out of courtesy to his wife, say he repented to having married her, he would not do it again. But he had had enough; a few years later he left the Quakers and joined the Unitarians. Elizabeth, or Bessy as he called her, despite being 'very small and compact', became a tower of strength in the family, dealing with William's many illnesses and money problems, supporting his reforming work and living to the ripe old age of 93. The secret of her longevity was apparently to take to her bed when things got on top of her and sleep for two days.

Richard, meanwhile, married Hannah Mary Reynolds, a half cousin who made her mark in British publishing in 1844 by writing what purport-

Slaves working on a cotton plantation in America. William Rathbone V regarded the cotton business as 'volatile and speculative' but did little to open up new avenues of trade, preferring to pursue political and charitable projects above business interests.

Elizabeth Greg, William Rathbone V's wife, was the daughter of a prosperous mill-owner who owned Quarry Bank Mill at Styal in Cheshire.

ed to be the diary of a lady during the Civil War. *Lady Willoughby's Diary* was printed by Longmans to look like the real thing, and was assumed by many readers to be that. When the deception was discovered there was a furore, but such was the readers' appetite for more that she went on to write a sequel. Richard retired from the firm in 1835 with what his nephew described as 'a very moderate fortune'.

William V's lively public career, which lasted 40 years, had a more domestic focus than his father's, and tracked the big liberal causes of the age. He pursued it with characteristic Rathbonian vigour, adding to his campaigning energies a sharp tongue which made him appear more formidable than he really was, and a considerable slice of the Rathbone fortune, which was one reason why the family's wealth declined.

The end of the Napoleonic Wars in 1815 allowed Britain to turn its attention back to its own condition, and it found poverty, injustice and suffering on a huge scale, prompting the formation of many reform movements. These invariably pitted the upcoming Whigs and Liberals against the entrenched Tories. Liverpool was typical in this: the top merchants and burghers who ran the town were mostly Tories who were more alert to their commercial interests than to social deprivation. The Peterloo Massacre in neighbouring Manchester in 1819, when dozens of demonstrators were killed or wounded in a cavalry charge, may have shocked them, but it also hardened their resolve to resist 'agitators'. True to character, William V protested against the massacre, for which he won an entry in the notorious Black Book of Lord Castlereagh, the minister most often blamed for the tragedy, as 'Dangerous, done nothing yet'.

William V became chairman of the Reform Association and Liberal Party in Liverpool, a position he held for nearly 30 years. This marked him out as a reformer, or troublemaker depending on your point of view, for which he had to put up with the same opprobrium as his father. However, he had an early and shocking experience of political unpopularity. In 1812, at the age of 25, he was present when Spencer Perceval, the prime minister, was assassinated in the

Quarry Bank Mill and Styal Estate, founded by Samuel Greg in 1784, is owned by the National Trust and has been restored to show the working life of the mill in the early years of the Industrial Revolution.

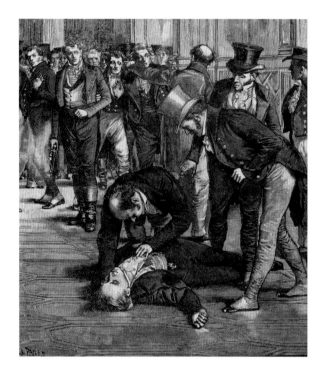

Spencer Perceval, prime minister, lies dying after being shot by John Bellingham, 1812.

lobby of the House of Commons by a deranged bankrupt. His distraught mother broke the news to his brothers in a letter which contained the agonising thought that 'had the hand of the poor lunatic trembled or varied ever so little from his aim, your Brother might have recd the shot which proved so instantly fatal to Spencer Perceval...'

William V's dearest cause was reform of the electoral system, which was deeply corrupt with Liverpool among the rottenest of the rotten boroughs. According to Eleanor Rathbone, the cost of a vote in Liverpool rose from a traditional five shillings (to make up for a lost day's work) to around £40 in the election of 1830. William, who had witnessed the problem as treasurer of an earlier election fund, attacked it head on, attending endless rallies and travelling up and down to London – all at his own (or the firm's) expense. To make his point, William V stood as a parliamentary candidate himself in the 1831 election so as to be able to 'demand the booths', that is, require that enclosed polling stations be set up around the constituency. This cut the time taken for the election and made it more orderly, reducing the expense and the scope for bribery.

William was not elected, no surprise, because he was standing against General Gascoigne, the incumbent senior MP for Liverpool who had been instrumental in scuppering earlier reform initiatives, and was supported by traditional Liverpool interests. William was even hissed on the 'Change. But eventually the tide of opinion turned. In 1832 Parliament passed the first of the great reform acts which extended the franchise and redistributed seats to get rid of rotten boroughs. When the Municipal Reform Act was passed in 1835 introducing similar changes at the local level, William's campaigning role was finally recognised and feted by his home town. The Liverpool Corporation, always keen on grand gestures, presented him with a magnificent set of silver plate, and pressed him to stand for mayor. Though initially reluctant, he accepted the position in 1837. This was also the year in which he laid the foundation stone for St George's Hall, the grandest municipal building in Liverpool. The hall stands to this day and is widely recognised as one of the finest examples of neo-classical architecture in the world.

In 1832 cholera reached England, possibly on a ship from India. Liverpool, with its squalid living conditions, was badly hit. The fact that cholera was a water-borne disease was not known for another 30 years, but bad sanitation clearly played a part, and there was a lot of that in Liverpool. William V helped raise forces to combat it, and in this he was greatly aided by the wife of one of his cotton porters, Kitty Wilkinson, who heroically nursed the sufferers and set up facilities in her own cellar to disinfect the linen of those who died. Once the epidemic receded, Kitty allowed her cellar to continue to be used as a wash house. This was found to be so useful that it led to the establishment of public baths and wash houses in Liverpool. Although William commended her services to the corporation, listing in detail the number of sheets, blankets and items of clothing she had washed, she received little in the way of thanks. Birrell notes: 'In a real history of Liverpool, Kitty Wilkinson would have a place above General Gascoigne, to whom, in this very year of cholera, repentant Liverpool presented its inevitable dinner service of plate with a suitable inscription.'

Another of William's campaigns focused on education in Liverpool, already a hornet's nest because of the growing religious divide between native Protestants and immigrant Catholics. But this was one of his less successful endeavours. As a member of a committee appointed to look into Liverpool's schooling, he was party to a policy that would have made schools non-sectarian: children received their education together and split up only at the end of the day for religious classes. But this provoked a sharp reaction from Protestants who accused Liverpool of driving the Bible out of school altogether, and the initiative collapsed. This was a special disappointment to his wife Bessy who was a school manager and backed William's work. William did, however, go on to support famine relief for the Irish.

Of all the campaigns that William fought, the one closest to his business interests was the Liverpool & Manchester Railway. This pioneering project to link the two great business centres of the North West was to become the world's first inter-city scheduled railway line carrying both goods and passengers. (The earlier Stockton & Darlington railway, opened in 1825, did not run a full service.)

For once, William V was firmly on the side of his Liverpool fellows: the opposition lay with the land-owners of the great estates through which the railway was to pass, and other threatened interests such as the turnpike and canal companies. The leader of the Liverpool campaign was James Cropper, with William and Richard Rathbone in support, plus dozens of wealthy businessmen and merchants from the two cities who were prepared to put up the money, initially around £400,000. After a long battle, parliamentary consent was given in 1826, and the project was completed four years later at a cost of £700,000. The railway transformed commerce in the North West by providing cheap and reliable transport between the region's largest manufacturing centre and its port, and handed its shareholders a handsome reward on their investment. Only five years later, the railway arrived from London, and the Lime Street terminus was built.

As William V slid into old age, the unpopularity

A cartoon by George Cruikshank lambasting the officials at the Central Board of Health in London for their complacency in dealing with the cholera epidemic that swept the country in 1832. Liverpool was badly hit with nearly 5,000 cases and 1,523 deaths.

William Rathbone V in his later years.

generated by his campaigns and irascible nature began to fade, and he ended his life in a warm glow of public appreciation, a grand old man still slightly daunting and clothed in the fashions of a bygone age – as late life photographs (the first of a William Rathbone) show us. In a symbolic move, the town council reinstated the portrait of him which had been removed from the Town Hall and given to the Mechanics' Institute, and put up a statue to him in Sefton Park. But his campaigning efforts had drained his health and his wealth, and left both in a sorry state. In 1868, when he was 80, a gallstone condition put him in great pain. His doctors told him he could have an operation to remove the stone, though it might be fatal. He decided to have the surgery, but died a few days afterwards. He had however lived long enough to see a new generation take the family firm in hand and open up new horizons.

William Rathbone V and his brother, Richard, backed the Liverpool & Manchester Railway which opened in 1830. It was the world's first major public railway; it ran to a timetable, carried passengers and freight, and provided a commercial and social link between the two cities. The opening was marred by William Huskisson, the Member of Parliament for Liverpool, being run over by George Stephenson's locomotive the 'Rocket' and thereby earning the unfortunate distinction of being the world's first railway passenger fatality. In 1836, Lime Street Station, Liverpool (shown here), opened for trains from London.

Greenbank – the Rathbone family home

When William Rathbone IV took on Greenbank in 1788 as a country retreat, it was a farmhouse with a garden, orchards and an ornamental lake belonging to Lord Sefton, the local grandee – a good place to escape the growing tumult and squalor of Liverpool. The Sefton estates were three miles outside the town, but still within easy travelling distance of the Rathbones' waterfront business. It soon became the centre of Rathbone family life.

When William died in 1809, he left Greenbank to his wife Hannah with instructions that she should rebuild it as she thought fit. Acting on this command, Hannah set about improving the house in the fashionable Strawberry Hill 'Gothick' style, giving it an imposing stone façade with plenty of cast iron work, probably manufactured at the Darby works in Coalbrookdale.

Hannah survived her husband by 30 years and in that time gave Greenbank a name for generous hospitality. One of Greenbank's most distinguished visitors was John James

Audubon, the American ornithologist and painter, who arrived in Liverpool in 1826 with an introduction to the Rathbones, and was welcomed to Greenbank where he stayed for several weeks. His diaries are full of ecstatic references to the family, the house and its gardens, and the natural surroundings. He was particularly fond of Hannah whom he describes as 'Lady Rathbone' or a 'Queen Bee reigning over Greenbank'. On August 14th, he wrote: 'This day I have passed with the delightful Rathbone family at Greenbank; I have been drawing for Mrs Rathbone and after dinner we went through the greenhouse and the jardin potager. How charming is Greenbank and the true hospitality of these English friends.' Audubon also spent much time with William V, to whom he presented a copy of his greatest work *Birds of America* inscribed with the words 'To William Rathbone Esq from his ever thankful, respectful and most obliged friend, the Author'. The book is still in the family's possession.

Other distinguished visitors included

One of William Rathbone V's American captains was Paul Cuffee, the first black captain to sail a ship into Liverpool. He was invited to dine at Greenbank and a portrait of him hung at Greenbank for many years.

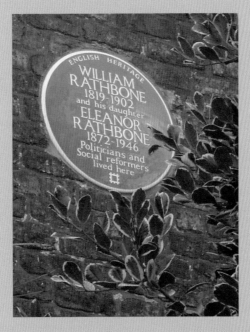

Robert Owen, the utopian reformer, Dorothea Dix, the Florence Nightingale of the American Civil War, and Paul Cuffee, one of the first American black sea captains to sail his ship into Liverpool. His portrait hung for many years at Greenbank.

Hannah was, however, overcome with guilt at the amount of money she had spent on the house, and decided to give it to her son, William V, having built herself a smaller cottage in the grounds.

Under William V, Greenbank continued its tradition of hospitality, extending it to include transatlantic passengers and ship captains who found themselves marooned by delayed sailings. By now it was quite a substantial household. Records from 1841 show that besides the family it housed six servants including a Swiss governess, a cook, a stableman and three house servants.

When William V died in 1868, his widow Elizabeth Greg invited William VI to move in with his family, which they did, adding further rooms and a conservatory. Greenbank went through another heyday as William VI used it to entertain in grand Victorian style, and

pursue his good works, including playing a major role in the foundation of University College, Liverpool, which in 1903 became the University of Liverpool.

By the end of the 19th century, though, Greenbank's heyday was approaching an end. Liverpool's wealthiest classes had begun to build mansions which far exceeded it in scale and opulence. The expanding city had also reached Sefton Park: Greenbank was no longer in the country but in the suburbs and, before a few more years had passed, within the city itself.

When William VI died in 1902, Greenbank was occupied by his second wife Emily until her death in 1918 when it passed to her daughter Evelyn and her husband Hugh Rathbone. The house had, by now, become difficult to maintain, and had lost its rural character. Hugh, who was closely involved with the university, came up with the idea of presenting it to that institution because it was, in a sense, its birthplace, and also because the house and grounds might be of value. Sydney Jones, the university's treasurer, welcomed the idea and suggested that Greenbank might be used as a residence for the vice-chancellor.

Starting in 1939, the Greenbank property was transferred bit by bit to the university by Hugh's children who continued to occupy it until 1944 when the transfer was complete. It had been in the family for 156 years.

In the 1960s, Greenbank was converted into a club for university staff and students and still stands amid lawns and trees, though with a rather unloved look and modern university buildings steadily encroaching.

In 2004 Greenbank came back into the spotlight when Rathbones launched its specialist ethical investment service for private investors and trustees wishing to ensure that their investments take full account of their environmental, social and ethical concerns: it is called Rathbone Greenbank.

Liverpool's fifth Custom House was built on the site of the Old Dock and opened in 1839. It was regarded as one of the finest buildings in Britain. Badly damaged in the Second World War, Liverpool Council chose to demolish the building rather than restore it.

THE GLORY DAYS OF EMPIRE

5

1840–1902

The neglect of the Rathbones business in the early 1800s due to William V's outside interests and his brother Richard's indifference left it in a very sorry state. We have seen how caution caused Rathbones to miss out on the boom in transatlantic trade that followed the American war of 1812. It must have seemed to their fellow merchants on the Liverpool waterfront that Rathbones was a spent force. Fortunately for the family, the new generation turned out to possess Rathbone vigour in plenty, and they were able to give the firm a fresh, though as it turned out, final burst in the merchanting business. After all, these were the glory days of Empire when Britain ruled the waves and seemed to have a God-given right to the riches of the world, many of which passed through Liverpool and propelled it to the peak of its greatness. It was an opportunity for the Rathbones to span the globe, and they took it.

Emily Rathbone, second wife of William VI.

William VI, painted by Sir William Richmond.

The heir to the business, William VI, seemed destined to be a player in this grand new age, born as he was in the same year as Queen Victoria, in 1819, and dying only a year after her in 1902. In the photographs we see a hard, even humourless face framed by mutton-chop whiskers, though his oil portrait does contain the hint of a smile, and we are told that he enjoyed snuff and hot buttered toast. Not an easy man, by all accounts, but one who got things done.

William VI was certainly the greatest of the 'WRs', measured by what he did for Rathbones and

for the nation: his imprint on both was profound. But he had a tricky start in life. He was a precocious, difficult child. The anecdotes of his early years are plentiful: he teased his elder sister and pulled her hair, and was twice whipped by his father. He also incited his sister to rebel against an inept governess, for which he was bundled off to school at the age of four. In his teens, still a troublemaker, he was sent to a bigger school in Everton where he kicked against the pettiness of the rules and persuaded the headmaster that boys would behave better if they were trusted more. 'This was

Samuel Greg Rathbone and William VI joined the family firm in 1842 and are credited with transforming the business. Samuel, shown here, served as a partner until 1885.

and built on his language skills by sending him to Heidelberg for a year to study history and law. Here, William VI learnt the habit of hard work but was appalled by the way 'the heavy hand of government' seemed to reach into all corners of German life and stultify creativity and freedom. This kindled in him the view, central to his later life in public affairs, that liberalism and democracy must lie at the heart of a just society.

His horizons soon widened further. On his return to England he joined Baring Brothers in their London office which was run by an American, Joshua Bates. Banks and merchant houses had a tradition of taking in each others' heirs for training and also to cement future links. Bates invited William to join him on a four-month tour of America, which William eagerly accepted. In the spring of 1841 he stepped aboard Isambard Kingdom Brunel's new paddle steamer the *Great Western* in Bristol with his father's advice ringing in his ears: 'Avoid the Slave Question!' The trip marked a milestone in Rathbones' evolution: despite the firm's extensive foreign interests, no member of the family had yet ventured abroad to inspect them. He and Bates travelled widely and according to William's account, met 'the best men from all parts of North America', including President John Tyler who threw a party for them in the White House. What struck William most about America was the mood of protectionism he encountered everywhere, an outcome of the severe depression the country was going through following a succession of big bank failures. The experience cemented his belief in free trade, not only as a commercial imperative but as a bulwark against monopoly and political extremism.

Soon after his return to England, he and his brother Samuel joined Rathbones and in time became partners. But in 1842 the firm was in dire straits. Their father, William V, had lost interest and their uncle Richard had already retired. More serious was the fact that the American business, once the heart of the firm, was in tatters because of poor management and the depressed state of the American economy. The collapse in cotton prices which accompanied the Amercian recession rapidly spilled over into the textile market and plunged Lancashire, too, into a recession which lasted four years, from 1839 to 1843.

William knew that things were bad because his

done,' he later wrote, 'and during my last half year at the school, it was remarkably free from disorder or mischief of any kind'. He was clearly someone who understood human nature.

There was to be no spell at Oxford for William VI, who admitted that he wasted most of his time at school and learnt little, apart from French and German. But he did emerge with a 'distinct desire for knowledge' and 'an ambition to maintain the good name of the family, and to fill at least a useful and respectable place in the world'. His father groomed him for business by placing him as an apprentice with a small firm of merchants where he spent three dispiriting years copying letters, running errands and helping out in the warehouses. But at least he gained a sense that the Rathbones were a bit special: his fellow workers all assumed that he would inherit great wealth and had no real need to work. 'I spared no pains to get rid of this belief ... for I knew this would be fatal to my being trusted with business.' The truth, of course, was that the family were not rich at all.

His father wanted him to see more of the world

father had told him before he went to America that 'we are living from hand to mouth, or rather mouth to hand for it is all going out and little coming in'. On examining the books, he discovered just what this meant: profits for the previous ten years had averaged only £10,000 and the firm's capital had shrunk to £40,000. The next three years were to be even worse: profits slumped to an average of £243 a year, which cannot have paid a living wage to the two young partners.

But William and Samuel, then aged 23 and 19, threw themselves into the business with the enthusiasm of youth. Fortunately, they made a good working pair: William had the drive and optimism, Samuel the steady hand and business skills. And fortunately, too, new opportunities were opening up.

The key to the impressive growth that Rathbones enjoyed over the 28 years that William and Samuel ran the business was William's determination that Rathbones should be 'amongst the swallowers rather than the swallowed'. Despite his young age, he had already seen too many firms fail through lack of competence and ambition, and his father had advised him: 'To small capitals and commerce, I fear the time is gone by.'

Two important developments in Britain's overseas trade took place over this period. In 1833 the monopoly of the East India Company on trade with the Far East was abolished, and in 1846 the Corn Laws' punitive tax on grain imports was repealed. William could see the opportunities these presented and he formulated what Sheila Marriner, the chronicler of this period of Rathbones' history, called 'a grand design' to grow the firm as never before. A stronger foreign presence was clearly required, and William planned visits to America, China and India to create a network of agents for a global Rathbones business.

One of his objectives was to offset the difficulties of the American trade by opening up promising new markets elsewhere. As a first step, he dispatched Samuel, barely 20 years old, to China to explore the possibilities. The Treaty of Nanking had just been signed in 1842 establishing the five so-called Treaty Ports for British trade, and there was a rush of interest. The openings for a firm like Rathbones plainly

When Samuel Rathbone visited China in the 1840s he was very excited by the prospect of importing tea and silk from the country. However, trade with China proved far harder than the Rathbones had imagined.

lay in tea and silk, the two commodities most in demand among Britain's increasingly wealthy middle classes, but there might be other things too. Samuel had an introduction to James Worthington, a schoolfellow of William's who was already out there trying to set up a trading house. The two joined forces and created a joint venture with branches in Shanghai and Canton called Rathbone, Worthington & Co. This marked another milestone in Rathbones' evolution: its first direct representation overseas. On his journey back, Samuel visited Ceylon and India where he called at Calcutta and Bombay and got a sense of the possibilities as well, though he returned with the view that there was 'much unsoundness' in India, particularly in Calcutta.

The new China trade, however, proved much more difficult to manage than they had expected. Chinese practices of corruption, smuggling and plain dishonesty seriously undermined the business, and made life very frustrating for Europeans posted in the Treaty Ports, who were not permitted to travel inland. Although the treaty promised access to markets, this could only be done through middlemen who were unreliable and generally did not speak English. One entry in Rathbone, Worthington & Co.'s books states simply that three of the company's creditors 'are missing for the present'. But the firm was more fortunate than a competitor who had his ledger stolen and presumed destroyed by a Chinese trader who owed him a large amount of money. There was the further problem of payment: the Chinese currency was volatile, and many traders preferred to settle their accounts in barter or even opium. This presented the more high-minded members of the trading community with a moral dilemma, including Rathbones. The articles of partnership for Rathbone, Worthington & Co. included a ban on the handling of opium, but this put a severe handicap on the business and it had to be informally relaxed, though at the cost of bitter internal wrangles.

Little could be done to improve trading conditions because of the xenophobia that pervaded China at the time, and this frequently exploded into episodes of violence, such as the Taiping Rebellion of 1851 into which Britain was dragged. Within only three years, Samuel was seriously disillusioned with the business he had helped set up. In 1849 he wrote to William VI: 'Of the China trade I am in despair

… Rathbone, Worthington & Co. are for the moment in the descendant.' The following year, William and Samuel decided that they had had enough so they shut down the Canton branch, and the Shanghai branch two years later. But they wanted to keep a foothold in China, and shifted their trading interests to local correspondents. This turned out to be a much better arrangement, if only because it distanced Rathbones from opium. Business began to pick up nicely too. Over the next four years, Rathbones' earnings from China amounted to £16,801 and continued to increase until 1863 when competition became much tougher. Most of this growth was built on tea for which Rathbones became one of the largest shippers to England, running a fleet of clippers (see box on pages 90–91).

One reason why the Rathbone brothers were keen to scale down in China was that America was picking up again, and resources were needed in that direction. In 1848 William VI was back in America and wrote to his father and brother: 'This country is a prosperous and advancing one, and I firmly believe any person conducting business here on proper principles … cannot fail to succeed.' There were many reasons for his optimism: cotton prices had strengthened and a new trading opportunity was about to appear in the form of corn after the repeal of the Corn Laws. With the return of economic prosperity, the threat of American protectionism had also receded.

In 1851 Rathbones decided to open up an agency in New York and gain a direct presence on the other side of the Atlantic, acting rather belatedly on the advice of Adam Hodgson who had reported during his visit there in 1820: 'I daily feel mortified at being compelled to enter into competition with those who, from having an establishment on this side of the water, possess advantages which we cannot compass.' The man they chose to run it was Henry Gair. The Rathbones had strong connections with the Gair family. Henry's father Samuel ran the Barings office in Liverpool, and it was he who had secured young William's position at Barings in London which led to his American tour. Henry's sister Lucretia was to become William's wife. Furthermore, Henry's parents were American-born, so he set out for New York with plenty of ready contacts in business and social circles – a natural choice for the job. The new agency was a rapid and enormous success.

Tea being loaded on junks in China. Rathbones' entry into the Chinese market was rocky initially but they became one of the largest shippers of tea to Britain.

The Rathbone ship, *Bosphorus*, entering the Mersey under full sail. A blue name pennant flies from the main mast but the artist misspells her name as 'Bosphorous'. At the foremast is the Rathbone house flag – an 'R' on a white band between two red bands. The ship was built in Canada and acquired by Rathbones in 1855. She sailed mainly to Bombay in India, picking up goods such as sugar, gunny cloth (sacking), jute, aloes and linseed.

Henry Gair was chosen to set up an office in New York in 1851. It was a huge success and in its first six years accounted for more than half the total earnings of Rathbones.

Its initial purpose was to strengthen Rathbones' contacts in North America and gather market intelligence. But the upturn in business was such that it soon took on more of the character of a branch, setting up deals and arranging finance. Trading volumes grew rapidly and, in its first six years, the agency came to account for more than half the total earnings of the Rathbones' business. This growth occurred once again largely on the back of cotton which defied William V's bearishness and remained strong. Between 1849 and 1863, Rathbones' earnings from cotton amounted to £127,231, making it much the most lucrative commodity they ever traded.

But this golden period was interrupted by the American Civil War in 1861 which cut off cotton supplies and resurrected the difficult question of slavery, the issue which sparked the conflict. Although, as we have seen, the Rathbones had long taken a principled stand against the slave trade, they differentiated, consciously or not, between trafficking in slaves and trading the produce of their labour.

Sugar and cotton both came from slave plantations and played an important part in Rathbones' business without causing qualms, even for William IV who was the most vociferous on the subject. But the issue of slavery lay at the heart of the Civil War and forced Rathbones to take up a clear position. When the war started, William and Samuel decided that they would no longer trade cotton on moral grounds, though, it has to be said that there was little to trade anyhow because the North had imposed a blockade on exports from the South. The two brothers instinctively supported the North as being the side fighting for human rights even though this once again put Rathbones in the minority in Liverpool where most of the merchants sided with the South, the source of their business.

The American Civil War was devastating for Lancashire. The halt in cotton supplies brought the mills to a standstill, throwing thousands out of work and into starvation conditions. The wealthy merchants of Liverpool felt they should do something to relieve the threat of famine. The mayor launched a drive to raise £20,000, but a small group of merchants including the Mellys and the Rathbones thought they could do better and eventually raised £100,000. The war was also divisive politically. The Laird shipyard across the Mersey in Birkenhead won orders to build three warships for the South, and the North made it plain that any support Britain gave to the Confederates would seriously damage relations. William was deeply concerned at this prospect and lobbied hard to get the government to stop the warships being delivered. One, the *Alabama*, managed to set sail and became a powerful weapon in the South's armoury. But the British government eventually bought the other two itself to stop them being deployed in the war.

Cotton was slow to get going again after the war finished in 1865. Although Rathbones started importing cotton as soon as it could, markets were very uncertain and demand in the Lancashire textile industry was deeply depressed by mill closures. In the ten years 1864–74, Rathbones lost nearly £30,000 on its cotton business and by the mid-1870s was beginning seriously to consider withdrawing from the market, which it finally did in 1875, though with much regret on William's part.

But for the business as a whole, all was far from lost. The repeal of the Corn Laws delivered its

American Civil War, the Battle of Gettysburg, 1863. The battle is frequently cited as the turning point of the war with up to 51,000 casualties over three days. The Rathbones sided with the North but the majority of Liverpool's merchants favoured the South.

promise of a surge in the grain market, in which Rathbones already had a presence. This business dated from 1839 when an Ulster brewer and distiller called Ross T. Smyth came over from Derry to Liverpool to set up a dealership in grain, a commodity which he knew a lot about with his beverage background. He took an office in Castle Street close to Rathbones, and the two firms began to do business. The grain trade at that time was desultory because of the Corn Laws, and William V was considering getting out of it. But the access that Smyth opened

up for Rathbones to the milling trade gave it fresh impetus, and the two firms decided to set up a new firm to work the relationship. It took the name Ross T. Smyth & Co. with Smyth and William V as its partners, and its offices in the Rathbones building. The new venture swiftly showed its paces, and eventually became one of Britain's leading grain merchants with five offices at home and eight abroad. It acted for Rathbones' grain business for nearly 50 years.

The grain trade had its ups and down, netting

Rathbones £10,500 in profits from 1849 to 1853, but losing it £6,700 over the next four years. But crucially it came into its own during the American Civil War when the North stepped up grain exports to pay for its campaign. In 1862 Rathbones raised the authorisation for the New York Agency from £5,000 worth of grain a week to £10,000, and upped imports from Canada as well. One factor speeding up the export of North American grain was the expansion of the rail network: this replaced canal and river transport which, aside from being slower, was liable to be iced up in winter. From 1864 to 1868, grain profits were £15,800, rising to £18,000 in the four years after that.

In the opposite direction, Rathbones shipped a variety of goods to America, including traditional manufactures from industrial Britain. The relaxation of navigation laws also widened the opportunity to transport goods between third countries. This enabled the firm to ship China tea and silk, and Brazilian coffee directly to America, for example. In fact, Sheila Marriner's research uncovered an astonishing range of goods moving across the Atlantic under the Rathbones flag: salt, railway iron and lead from Britain; hides from Calcutta, Montevideo and Buenos Aires; rice from the Far East; wool from South Africa; sugar from Cuba, Madras and Manila; hemp from Manila; and gunny cloth (a kind of sacking), jute, aloes and linseed from India.

On the homeward journey, Rathbones' ships carried, in addition to cotton and grains, quantities of hops, guano, lard, apples, sugar, rice, tobacco, and something very new called petroleum.

Another geographical shift in Rathbones' business took place in mid-century. When William drew up his master plan he recognised that while Liverpool handled the goods, many of them ended up in markets located in the City of London, particularly tea which was now a key commodity for Rathbones. He therefore decided in 1851 to open a London office to which he appointed a tea taster, a Mr Thistlethwaite, to oversee the brokers and see that they did not 'slaughter' the produce just to get rid of it. But tea was seasonal, and the office started dealing in other goods such as jute, sugar and coffee to fill fallow periods. Being close to the country's banking markets, it also became the focus of Rathbones' financial affairs. The office proved so useful that it was expanded to include a dealing capability and

eventually became a fully-fledged branch under the management of a new partner, William Lidderdale (see box on page 95).

Getting Rathbones back on its feet and expanding it at such an ambitious pace required a supreme effort on the part of William VI and Samuel. Looking back on the period, William VI described the first five years as 'very uphill work' when they scarcely took a holiday. But their labours began to pay off, and the firm soon became very prosperous. When the brothers' father died in 1868 William said: 'We had not only made a very comfortable capital for ourselves, but more than trebled my father's capital in the business.' In fact the accounts for 1871 show that the house distributed a record dividend that year of £80,500. The following year its capital was estimated at £600,000, excluding the Rathbones interest in Ross T. Smyth & Co. This compared with £40,000 when the brothers took the business on in 1842, exactly 30 years earlier. It was, according to Marriner who reconstituted the firm's accounts, 'the period of maximum prosperity' for the family firm.

Although William VI might have felt that he was making up for the shortcomings of the older generation with his success, he took the exact opposite line. If he had inherited a thriving business and huge riches, he said, 'this would have thrown up a great temptation on his children to rest upon their father's labours and to live upon the result'. Instead, he says, the poor condition of the firm and family fortune 'was the making of us as men of business'.

The rapid pace of expansion also required structural changes to the firm. In 1838, shortly before the two brothers took over, Rathbones had left its historic Cornhill site by the docks for offices at 16 South Castle Street in the town centre. In 1852 the firm moved again, to 24 Water Street, and 20 years after that to Drury Buildings, 21 Water Street, where they remained until 1911. The two brothers also took on new partners. Henry Gair, who opened the New York agency, became a partner in 1854, and his successor in New York, William Lidderdale, joined the partnership in 1863 when he returned to England to run the London house. A further partner, Thomas Twist, had joined in 1847, but little is known about him. But even with extra manpower, the strain was telling. William's dynamism became rather trying for Samuel. In 1854, Samuel wrote to William VI and Henry Gair complaining that the

In 1854, American businessman Cyrus Field developed plans to lay a telegraph cable from America to Newfoundland, and from there to Ireland. It was a huge undertaking, with many setbacks but in 1858 the first official message – from Queen Victoria to the American President James Buchanan – crossed the Atlantic. The 2,500 miles of cable were laid by Brunel's steamship, the *Great Eastern*.

workload was too heavy and complicated, and unless something was done about it, the efficiency of the firm and the health of the partners could be damaged. This eventually led to a decision to divide responsibility among the partners, one dealing with the China trade (Samuel), one with the American (William), and one with finance (Lidderdale in London).

The emphasis from then on was on opportunity, but safe opportunity because, for all his drive, William was a cautious man. He had learnt by experience that the losses from speculative investments invariably wiped out the profits from sound ones. He later wrote: 'At the commencement of my business experience I saw that those businesses produced ultimately the best results which required patience and labour, and where people were content with an apparently moderate profit. Whereas, in businesses which occasionally gave large profits and large losses, the net final result was infinitely less satisfactory.' One consequence of this caution was that Rathbones turned down a merger approach from one of its waterfront competitors, John Swire & Sons, in 1872. It would have made a good match because Swires specialised in the China trade and had an excellent business in tea and silk, but needed better access to the American market where Rathbones was strong. However, the cautious Rathbones found

Swires' business style too speculative and turned the offer down, which was probably a mistake. This was one of the early indications that the Rathbones were losing the adaptability that had served them so well in the past, and presaged one of the most difficult periods in Rathbones' history.

William VI was probably content to ease the pace because he, too, was feeling the strain for business and personal reasons. In 1847 he had married Lucretia Gair, Henry's sister, and they moved across the Mersey to a home in New Brighton to breathe cleaner air and raise a family. In 1852, his father reminded him that it was time to follow the Rathbone tradition of public service so William threw himself into local politics, becoming chairman of the Liberal Party and a member of the Dock and Harbour Board. He also took on the chairmanship of the American Chamber of Commerce in which capacity he gave a banquet in 1858 for Cyrus West Field, the pioneer of the transatlantic telegraph cable which was to transform Liverpool's merchanting business, for good and ill. During the meal a commemorative cablegram was received from America. But the days of instant communication were still a few years off. The insulation on Field's cable turned out to be faulty and it had to be replaced soon afterwards; it was not until 1868 that reliable communications were achieved.

But the strain of taking on these new duties while still running the business began to undermine William's health. In 1856 he suffered a breakdown from which he had difficulty recovering. Two years later, still in poor health, his doctor advised him to take a full year off, so he and Lucretia went to live in Cumloden in rural south-west Scotland. William recovered, but unfortunately Lucretia's health, always frail, broke down and the following year she died. This was a devastating blow for William VI who had frequently written lovingly of Lucretia's qualities. But it opened up the phase of his public career for which he is now best remembered, the creation of district nursing.

William was so impressed by the care that his wife received from her nurse, Mary Robinson, that he engaged her for three months to attend to the poor of Liverpool who did not have access to home nursing. He knew of their plight because one of his charitable works had been to call door to door in the poor districts to collect savings for the Provident

Society. At the time, nursing was available only on a paid private basis, or through the overloaded public hospitals. After only one month Mrs Robinson appeared before William in tears to say that she could no longer bear the misery she had encountered in her work, and asked to be released from her engagement. William pressed her to complete the three months, after which Mrs Robinson appeared once again, bright-eyed, saying that she felt she was doing so much good that she would never return to private nursing. William formed the idea of creating a corps of district nurses to carry this work further and got in touch with Florence Nightingale who was pressing for reform of Britain's nursing service at the national level. Nightingale advised William to set up a training scheme for nurses at the Liverpool Royal Infirmary. The idea was not welcomed by the Infirmary which had views of its own on caring for the poor and, besides, had no facilities to train or house

district nurses. Undaunted, William got himself elected to the hospital's management committee and offered to bear all the costs of setting up a scheme, provided the hospital would give it a fair chance. The scheme was a rapid success. Within two years the hospital had a team of district nurses, and the service was soon extended to the whole of Liverpool, and eventually nationally. It was an extraordinary achievement, which received the personal recognition of Queen Victoria (though he was never honoured). Florence Nightingale wrote to him: 'I am very thankful to hear that the Liverpool nursing work is going so well', and contributed an introduction to a report he later wrote called *A Sketch of the History and Progress of District Nursing.*

William's generosity in offering to pay for the scheme was prompted by the views he held about wealth and philanthropy. As we have seen, he began life with only modest financial means and with the

After the death of his wife, Lucretia, in 1859, William VI set up a training scheme for nurses at the Liverpool Royal Infirmary.

Hampstead N.W

Sept 26 /64

Dear Mr. Rathbone

I must plead my usual excuse for not having thanked you before for your beautiful ferns & flowers & paper.

I do not think you need be troubled about not having the all the accommo-dation ⨯ Ship Lanes think desirable. She herself informed me of it – but her chief trouble was

⨯ Workhouse Inf.

A woman suffering from rheumatism in Rathbone Street. This sketch was drawn by Lucie Devenish, a district nurse. William Rathbone VI's scheme for training nurses was so successful that it was used as a model throughout the country.

One of the many letters from Florence Nightingale to William Rathbone VI.

conviction that people should create wealth for themselves rather than inherit it. He was also by nature frugal and uninterested in luxury. Nonetheless, he believed that a man's standing in society – and particularly Liverpool society – was judged by how successful he was at managing his own affairs, and for a businessman that meant how much money he had. So it was important for his business credibility and self-esteem that he be seen to amass wealth, hence his feelings of satisfaction at the material success he achieved through his business. Indeed, he related that he was once tipped off about a forthcoming issue of shares in a French railway company that was bound to rise to a premium on the open market. He bought £1,000 worth and they immediately rose 50 per cent, giving William a nice £500 profit which he pocketed with a mixture of contentment and guilt.

William VI paid his staff generously, and incentivised them with bonuses and profit-sharing. In 1856, a year in which the firm made moderate profits, the salary bill amounted to £1,834, and bonuses £1,000. The following year saw a 50 per cent increase in profits and, although the salary bill went down slightly to £1,612, the firm paid out over two and a half times as much in bonuses: £2,755. The firm's agents and correspondents, such as tea-tasters and silk inspectors, also got gratuities out of the profits.

But there were limits. William once wrote: 'My feeling with a merchant was that when he got over £200,000 he was too rich for the Kingdom of Heaven.' In later life when he had become very wealthy, he propounded the view that once a man had earned enough to finance his primary responsibility, namely his family, anything else he owned was held on trust for the happiness and welfare of his fellow men. This was not just a philanthropic view. William had observed that the marginal advantage to a person of a growing income declined over his lifetime: there was steadily less use that he could personally make of the extra money. A man should therefore apportion a rising share of his income to public objects, possibly as much as half. He was also guided by his religious views and his close connection with the non-conformist church. He took on the Unitarian faith of his father and attended its chapel in Renshaw Street where his brother-in-law, the Rev. John Thom, was the minister. Throughout his life he was

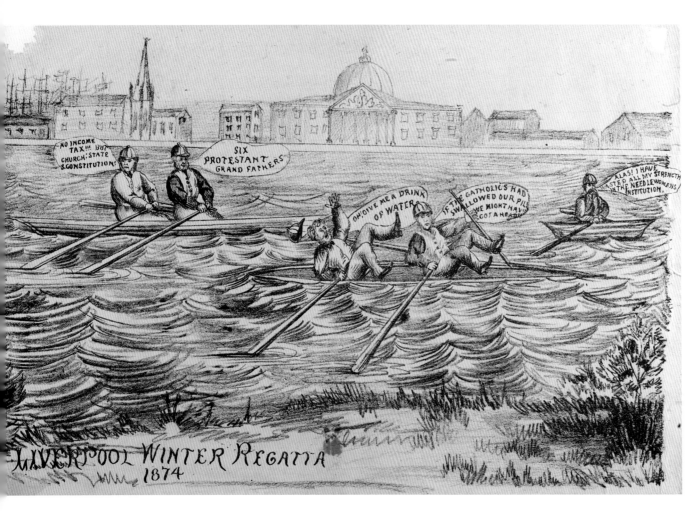

LIVERPOOL WINTER REGATTA 1874

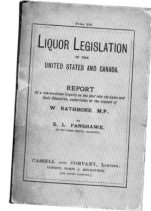

Report written by William Rathbone VI during his time as an MP.

interested in charitable works, though he applied a hard-nosed approach and usually checked out the recipient before handing over any money.

William VI got an opportunity to enlarge his role in public service when the local Liberal Party asked him to stand as a parliamentary candidate in the 1868 election. This he agreed to do after obtaining the opinion of friends and colleagues that far from sacrificing Liverpool's interests, he would be in a much better position to further them. William was elected and served as MP for Liverpool for 12 years, playing what his daughter Eleanor (later herself an MP) called 'an arduous, thorough and unostentatious' backbench role in a Parliament dominated by William Gladstone's first premiership. The political air was thick with domestic and foreign policy issues and William could take his pick: among the debates he chose were reform of the licensing laws (though an abstainer, he was against prohibition and commissioned a study of the US market), reform of the

bankruptcy laws (which he supported), further reform of parliamentary procedure and local government (also much in favour) and the introduction of a load line for seagoing ships, an issue of great interest to Liverpool. Following a series of ship losses, many caused by overloading, William's fellow MP Samuel Plimsoll was pressing for the introduction of compulsory load lines. The shipowning community strongly opposed further regulation, arguing that they were the best judges of seaworthiness, and William took their side. But he was onto a loser. The Merchant Shipping Act of 1876 introduced the Plimsoll Line which soon became a world marker.

In the 1880 election, William was persuaded to step down from his Liverpool seat and stand instead for South West Lancashire as part of a tactical repositioning of Liberal gunnery. But it misfired. William was defeated, though he was later re-elected as MP for Caernarvonshire where he served for another 13 years. However, his work in Parliament represented

Samuel Plimsoll, responsible for the Merchant Shipping Act of 1876 which set limits on ships' loads. William Rathbone VI, along with other shipowners, was opposed to Plimsoll's regulations. Below: A Plimsoll line in use today on the hull of a ship.

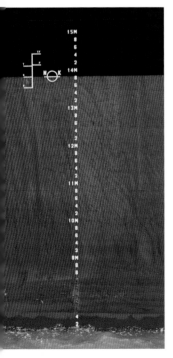

only a part of his public service. Back on Merseyside, he became president of the Liverpool Institute and supported the establishment of a college of higher education which was granted a charter as University College, Liverpool, in 1881 and became the University of Liverpool in 1903. In the 1880s he repeated the achievement by helping to set up the University College of North Wales in Bangor in his Caernarvon constituency. He was rewarded for his public service with a bronze statue outside St George's Hall in the heart of Liverpool.

While William was engaged in political life, the

Rathbones business began to falter. It missed William's drive, but there was also the familiar problem of an ageing generation failing to confront change. In her history of Rathbone Brothers, Lucie Nottingham writes of this period: 'Mercantile life was changing rapidly at this time. The heyday of the general merchant and the commission merchant, both trades in which Rathbones had excelled, was giving way to a world of increasingly stiff competition; of specialised broking firms and futures markets; of shipping lines; and of changed business practices brought about by the improved communications provided by steam and telegraph. It needed a flexible, determined and forward-looking organisation to cope with these changes – something that Rathbones was not.'

William was acutely aware of these pressures. His friend and China business colleague William Brown had written to him in 1866 observing that 'in every department we have somewhat allowed things to drift'. But it wasn't just new technology and new markets that were exposing the firm's weaknesses, it was the lack of common purpose among the partners, a loss of interest which grew as the years went by. William and Samuel began to fall out. In 1884, a year in which Rathbones lost £50,000, Samuel wrote to William: 'Considering how much time you have devoted to the service of the country, I think you might devote four or five days to the consideration of the firm's affairs at what I regard as "the crisis of its destinies".' Shortly afterwards Samuel retired from the firm. By then, William Lidderdale was increasingly involved with the Bank of England of which he had become a director in 1870, and William VI's heir William VII, born in 1849, was developing a successful career in London and showed little interest in returning to Liverpool, possibly to avoid a strong-willed father. Of William's other sons, Ashton the second eldest showed promise but died of blood poisoning in 1895. The third, Harry, had gone to live in Florence and the fourth, Edward, died in a boating accident in 1886. It was almost as if fate was taking a hand: for the first time in over 150 years there was no male Rathbone, let alone a William, ready to take the reins. The only hope was William VI's youngest son Frank by his second marriage, but in 1885 he was only ten years old.

William badly needed to find new blood to keep the firm going. In 1877 he lighted upon Arthur

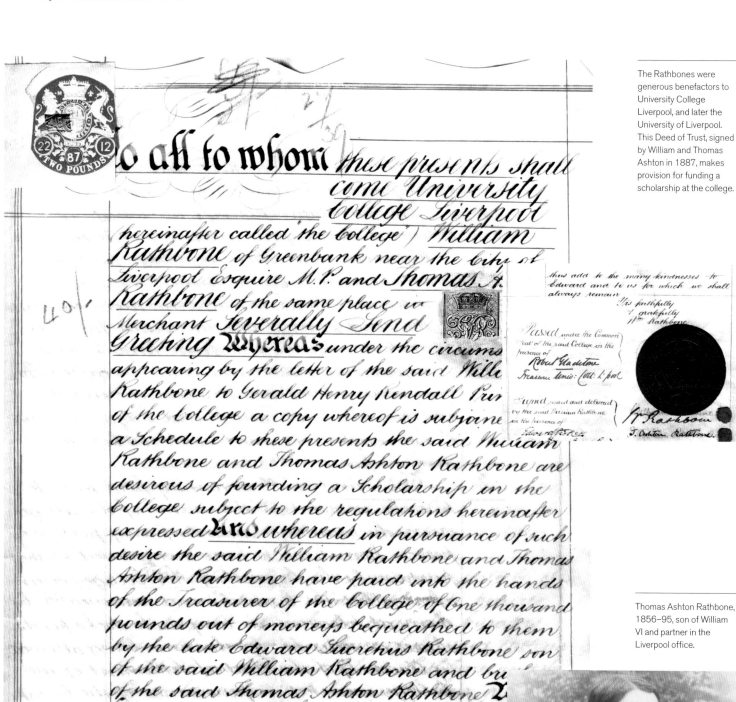

Thomas Ashton Rathbone, 1856–95, son of William VI and partner in the Liverpool office.

Towards Close of Day by Robert Dudley. This atmospheric view of Canada Dock in Liverpool captures the hustle and bustle of the port in the 1870s. Canada was Britain's major source of timber at this time.

Radford who was working in the grain trade with Ross T. Smyth and offered him a three-year trial with the promise of a partnership if it worked out. Radford was very much second best, and did not impress his new colleagues. However, three years later, no one else had appeared upon the scene and William felt obliged to deliver on his promise. Lidderdale wrote to William: 'Although we don't much care for him, it seems to me we had better take him.' Radford stayed with the firm for 25 years but never became close to the family.

In the last two decades of the century, Rathbones

fell into decline, just as it had at the end of the previous generation. A voluminous correspondence between William VI, Samuel, Lidderdale, Ashton, William VII and others over this period shows them all struggling for solutions, but none able to act decisively, a sign of advancing loss of will. There were sporadic attempts to develop a strategy. William favoured tea, silk, hemp and shipowning, all areas where he felt Rathbones had the advantages of good credit, market knowledge and ample capital. He conspicuously did not go for cotton which had become highly competitive and dominated by

Rathbones and ships

The history of Rathbones is inseparable from shipping. Rathbones built ships, owned them, hired them, handled them. For most of its early existence, the Rathbones yard on Merseyside was filled with the sight of sails, the sound of rigging and the smell of tar. When the Rathbones wrote letters to each other, they inquired after one another's health and went on to relate which ships were in port.

In the days of Williams II and III, Rathbones built ships and probably owned a few small ones. They also acted as Liverpool agents and repairers for shipowners in the Baltic and America, which gave them a lively business arranging voyages and charters, and handling cargo. In 1818 Rathbones was party to a big advance in shipping: the inauguration of the first scheduled monthly service across the Atlantic, between New York and Liverpool. The Black Ball Line ships were American-owned and Rathbones acted as British agents along with Cropper, Benson & Co. Up till then ships delayed their departure until they were full, which might take weeks, so a regular service provided certainty.

In his memoirs of early 19th-century Liverpool, William VI describes how ships used to gather in the Mersey, waiting as long as 30 days for a favourable wind. When it finally came, the estuary was so crowded with white sails that he felt he could cross it by stepping from deck to deck.

Rathbones' direct interest in shipping grew rapidly in the middle of the 19th century with the massive expansion of its overseas activities, particularly the China trade which was much less developed than the North Atlantic. One of the earliest large ships they owned, jointly with Cropper, Benson & Co, was the *Bengal* which became only the second ship to sail east

The Rathbone ship *Scawfell* pictured off Hong Kong at anchor with her sails stowed, 1858. She was a 'clipper' in the true sense, a relatively large vessel built primarily for speed, and made several record voyages between the East and Britain.

after the abolition of the East India Company monopoly on trade with China in 1833. Although it was fitted with gun ports, its pacifist Quaker owners insisted that it be equipped with dummy wooden guns to scare off would-be attackers.

The 19th century brought major changes to the shipping industry. One was the transition from individual ownership to 'lines': groups of ships running a regular service. In 1865 Rathbones teamed up with Lamport & Holt to form a shipping line to Latin America, and a few years later joined the Star Navigation Co. which ran between Britain and India.

In the 1860s, Rathbones became one of the largest importers of tea into Britain

and owned a fleet of clippers which plied the route between China and Liverpool. The largest, the *Bosphorus*, was 1,346 tons and 217 feet long. More famous was the smaller *Scawfell* which Rathbones owned from 1859 to 1871. The *Scawfell* held several records for the trip back from the East: in 1861 it made the journey from Macao to the Point Lynas lighthouse on Anglesey in 85 days. All this made Rathbones an important name in shipping, and for a while its earnings from ships were second only to those from its trade with China.

Another change was the advance from sail to steam. The first steamship puffed its way up the Mersey as early as 1815 where

Scawfell log book.

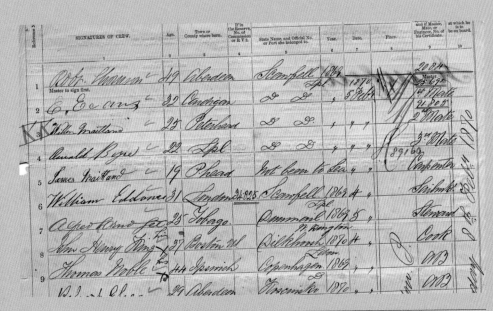

Scawfell records giving details of the crew on a voyage in 1870. All the crew appear to be able to sign their names in excellent writing and they come from around Britain: Ipswich, Aberdeen, Peterhead, London and Liverpool, as well as from further afield; Tobago and Boston. They include carpenters, sail makers, cooks, and 1st, 2nd and 3rd mates. Many of them had crewed on the *Scawfell* previously although by the carpenter it is noted that he has 'not been to sea'.

it plied an unromantic service between Liverpool and Runcorn. In 1837 Brunel launched his pioneering *Great Western* paddle steamer (on which William VI made his first journey to New York). Rathbones got into steam around 1860 through its partnership with Lamport. The advantage was greater certainty, though on the tea clipper routes sail still held the advantage of speed. William always favoured steam after he witnessed the *Great Western* run aground on a floating icefield and get itself off under its own power.

The growth of shipping was also fuelled by the boom in passenger services, particularly emigration for which Liverpool became the largest embarkation point in Britain, 'the floodgate of the world'. In 1851 Liverpool handled 160,000 passengers, three times as many as Le Havre and Bremen combined. Rathbones did not specialise in passengers like some other lines, but it carried them on its merchant ships and acted as agents for others.

To handle the booming shipping business, Liverpool regularly added more docks to the 'Old Dock' (which was filled in in the 1820s to make room for warehousing). These eventually stretched more than five miles in each direction along the Mersey

shore and were connected by an elevated railway. In the 1860s Hippolyte Taine, the French historian, visited Liverpool and described the granite-lined basins crowded with ships as like a leafless winter forest stretching as far as the eye could see. 'The spectacle of the Liverpool docks is, I think, one of the greatest in the whole world', he wrote.

But by the end of the 19th century, the economics of shipping were turning against smaller operators like Rathbones. Giant liners and cargo ships were appearing, the Suez Canal opened in 1869, and competition intensified. The Rathbones business was also losing its dynamism as the partners aged. In the 1880s, the firm decided to get out of shipping, and sold the business to their rivals Harrisons & Crosfield. It was the end of an era.

The *Bengal* was owned jointly by Rathbones and Cropper, Benson & Co. She was the second ship to sail from Liverpool to Calcutta after the abolition of the East India Company's monopoly, and carried wooden cannon to scare off the enemy.

William Rathbone VII visited China in the 1880s with his wife but he was not active in the Rathbones' business.

brokers rather than merchants. Samuel also favoured tea and shipping, and with some foresight added banking, which was to become a future Rathbones activity. But Samuel was by then despondent, believing that the days of traditional merchanting had been destroyed by 'permanent speculative gambling elements' introduced by rapid communications and easy money. In a move that symbolised the changes coming over the firm, Rathbones decided to sell its shipping business in the mid-1880s, having been advised by Alfred Holt, the Liverpool shipping magnate, that it was not big enough to compete in the new age.

A further problem was the rivalry between the Liverpool and London houses against a background in which the London market was booming and Liverpool was showing the first signs of decline. The

The Rathbones on holiday in Scotland, 1892.
Back row, left to right, William Rathbone VI, Emily, his second wife, and Eleanor, later a politician and social reformer.
Front row, left to right, Evie, Frank (with Nancy), Hugh (with Reynolds), Elsie.

Liverpool house continued to dominate the firm and hold the purse strings, but with the shift of key commodity markets to London, the firm's financial management now rooted in the City and the sale of key businesses like cotton and shipping, the house on the Thames felt it had risen above the one on the Mersey. In turning down a request by London for more capital in 1884, Samuel wrote: 'If two firms, or rather branches of that firm in two different towns, are to have a common profit and loss account, one or the other of them must be supreme and the other one a mere subordinate branch carried on by partners in the position of head clerks .... Neither of our branches will take this position.' Rathbones' insistence that Liverpool remain the heart of the firm was a sign of family pride, but it also betrayed a blindness to commercial reality. Hard though it must have been for Liverpudlians to see it, the city's business was beginning to shift elsewhere. Several of Rathbones' main competitors, Harrisons & Crosfield, Brown Shipley and Swires, had moved to London and beyond where they were to prosper.

The crisis between the two houses came to a head in the mid-1890s when London, with Lidderdale back in charge after his spell as Governor of the Bank of England, took to speculating in foreign stocks and lost a great deal of money. William, by now nearly 80 years old, insisted on a stop being put to the speculation and did his best to hush things up. In a memorandum in June 1897 headed 'Very confidential, please burn as soon as read' he castigates Lidderdale for his mismanagement and urges the unnamed recipient 'not to allude to losses or this letter to anyone: people exaggerate so much in excess of the reality when they hear of losses … and it might inflict much injury on us all'. It was a desperate moment for a man in the twilight of his life who had achieved so much.

William's first instinct was to shut the firm down and be shot of all the worry. But his colleagues at Ross T. Smyth, which was still in good financial health, urged him to keep going, though they were not willing to accept William's suggestion of a merger because they already had enough partners. This left William VI with little choice but to scale down the business and try to find it a new role. It was deeply painful, but it offered the only hope of survival. The ignominious retreat involved shutting

down the London office, which was done 'as quietly as possible' in 1898.

The glory days of Rathbones were over. The cotton was gone, as were the ships and the London tea. And soon William himself was gone. In his closing years he succumbed to an increasing number of maladies, and once again took refuge in Scotland where he trundled around in a pony-drawn invalid carriage and put his voluminous papers in order. He died on March 6th 1902. In accordance with his wishes, he was cremated, and his ashes buried in Toxteth Cemetery. His brother Samuel died the following year.

In an account of his life which he prepared for his children in 1894 (and from which many of the quotes in this chapter are taken), William described himself as 'simply an average Englishman of ordinary ability, but for that reason able to understand the wants of the day'. It was an excessively modest self-assessment, but one which could be equally applied to his private and his public lives.

Liverpool conferred its highest honour on William Rathbone VI by making him an Honorary Freeman of the city in 1891.

William Lidderdale: the man who saved Barings but almost destroyed Rathbones

The most famous partner in Rathbones was William Lidderdale who was Governor of the Bank of England during the Barings crisis of 1890. Lidderdale was born in 1832 in St Petersburg, Russia, where his father was the British chaplain. He was educated at Birkenhead and began work with Heath & Co., merchants who specialised in trade with Russia. Here he came to the notice of Rathbones who invited him to join the firm as cashier and later to run their agency in New York, which he did for six years. In 1863 he returned to Liverpool where he was made a partner and sent to head the firm's new office in London. This was a key appointment because he was responsible for the firm's considerable capital as well as its dealings in London markets such as tea.

Lidderdale quickly showed an aptitude for financial matters, and built a good knowledge of the workings of the City. His reputation rising, he was invited by the Bank of England to become a director in 1870. From there he went on to become deputy governor in 1887 and Governor in 1889. Lidderdale believed that the Bank should drop some of its aloofness and get closer to financial markets to gain more influence in City affairs, where he saw increasing signs of speculation. This stood him in good stead when the Barings crisis broke after he had been Governor less than a year.

Barings, one of the City's top merchant banks, lost large amounts of money speculating in Argentinian shares but its plight had to be kept secret to prevent a panic.

Lidderdale decided that Barings would have to be bailed out, but he needed Treasury backing for a loan. In order to obtain it without raising suspicions, he slipped out of a side door of the Bank and hailed a hansom cab to Whitehall where he was given 24 hours to put a rescue together. The promise of government money was enough to get other banks and merchant houses to join a guarantee fund which eventually totalled £17m. The guarantors included Rathbone Bros. & Co. which put in £50,000, and William Rathbone who chipped in £20,000 on his own account, his brother Samuel (£10,000) and his brother-in-law Henry Gair (£20,000). In fact Lidderdale leaned heavily on his Liverpool connections to raise the cash: among the 50 or so guarantors, more than a dozen came from the area, including Brown Shipley (£200,000) and Martins (£100,000). It took several years, but they all eventually got their money back, plus interest.

Lidderdale was much praised for his decisiveness. Among the letters of congratulation he received was one from the Chancellor of the Exchequer, Sir William Harcourt, saying: 'The Baring Guarantee was a bold and probably necessary stroke. It has ended well. May it never be repeated.'

But though Lidderdale emerged as the City's saviour, his later career is filled with lesser known ironies. After he left the Bank in 1892, he resumed his post as Rathbones' London partner where he engaged in heavy speculation in foreign shares and lost very large amounts of money, not just the firm's but his own as well. In 1897 he confessed to William VI in Liverpool: 'My capital has more than all gone.' The losses forced Rathbones to close its London office, and almost drove it out of business altogether. As a result of this fiasco, Lidderdale was obliged to buy himself out of the partnership, for which he needed to borrow £35,000. He found a grateful lender: Baring Brothers.

He died four years later, a poor man.

A FRESH START
1902–1988

I n the final years of his life, William VI, ageing, ill and exhausted, and without an obvious successor, was strongly inclined to shut the business down. Thanks to Lidderdale's costly mismanagement and the bewildering pace of change, the firm had completely lost its way. A memorandum from 1898 predicted that profits over the next three years were unlikely to be better than those of 1842–44, William's first years in the business, when they totalled a mere £730. William's last-ditch attempt to save Rathbones by merging it with Ross T. Smyth came to nothing. Furthermore, the 'reconstruction' that friends were urging on him would, William believed, merely renew rather than resolve the anxieties he had suffered on the firm's behalf for many years.

But even in these dire straits, William managed to summon the energy and determination to rescue Rathbones from extinction. In 1898 he decided that 'it would be wrong to throw away the position of a firm which had, for seven generations during nearly two centuries, afforded the means and opportunity of honourable maintenance and usefulness to our family and various friends and business connections'. Aged 80, he set about giving the firm a new start with fresh capital and a different strategy.

From his own personal fortune, he put up £20,000 in immediately available cash plus another £20,000 that was to be held in trust by Ross T. Smyth on the condition that the business 'be

William Gair Rathbone VII, William Rathbone VIII and William Rathbone VI, 1895.

The break in the family line

William VII is remembered as the first William Rathbone who did not run the family business. He was nonetheless an interesting and successful figure in his own right.

Born in 1849, he was educated at Rugby and Oxford and joined Rathbones in 1872 after a brief spell at Barings. He was sent to run the New York office in the 1870s where he married Blanche Luling, the daughter of German immigrants. William VI did not take to Blanche for some reason, and when the couple returned to England they decided to settle in London rather than Liverpool. Here William VII worked with William Lidderdale in the Rathbones office, and was partly responsible for the disastrous losses the firm suffered there. His personal debts were such that he had to be bailed out to the tune of £12,000.

However, after the office was closed in 1898, he prospered and became a leading City figure with directorships of several banks and the P&O Steamship Company, something

of which William VI also disapproved because he thought outside directorships distracted people from the main task.

William VII and Blanche played a leading role in London society, attracting a coterie of American cultural figures including Henry James and John Singer Sargent. William VII was also keen on music, befriending the Australian composer Percy Grainger who dedicated his pastiche 'Handel in the Strand'

William Rathbone VII with his family.

to him, and commissioning work from the young Frederick Delius. He and Blanche kept the family tree going by producing a son, William VIII, and through him a line which currently extends to William XII. William VII died in 1919.

His daughter lying on a giant water lily.

conducted on moderate and prudent lines', and that he be supplied with monthly accounts and half-yearly detailed statements. Henry Gair Rathbone, his third son, also agreed to put in £10,000, giving the 'new' firm a total of £50,000.

William's insistence that Rathbones move out of speculative trading hastened the shift away from most of its traditional markets and into new avenues which had been hinted at by Samuel a few years earlier: banking and financial services. William stipulated that Rathbones should engage in 'the management of investments and collections of dividends and investment funds for Trustees and others…', though he envisaged that it might also trade in commodities like wool 'without serious risk'. In other words, the new strategy was to be built largely on living off the Rathbone fat, looking after the money of family and friends, and handling the day-to-day administration of their financial affairs.

Given that his eldest son William VII was now happily ensconced in London and reluctant to move up to Liverpool, William VI entrusted this new business to his nephew, Samuel's son Robert Rathbone, and to Arthur Radford, the outside partner whom he had taken on back in 1877. He must have done this with considerable reluctance since he did not have a high opinion of Radford, and he had earlier described Robert as 'addicted to idling and dreaming'. In order to beef up the governance of the firm, William appointed two partners of Ross T. Smyth, his son-in-law Hugh Rathbone and Douglas Muir, as advisers with instructions to make regular visits and check on progress.

Rathbones thus underwent a profound transformation to face the challenges of a new century. But the traditions of an older age were hard to break, as may be gleaned from a light-hearted account of life in the Rathbones office penned some years later by William VIII who, fresh from Eton, worked there from 1902 to 1907.

William's account shows Robert to be the driving force, though with a style that mixed shrewdness with eccentricity. He had lost an eye playing polo as a young man and would discomfit visitors by removing the glass substitute and dropping it into his drink. This did not prevent him either continuing with his polo, or becoming a member of the early British skiing set.

'The staff consisted of Mr. John Boadle, head clerk and cashier. A stern disciplinarian of the old school. Short, greying beard, with every detail of each clerk's job in his head, and a reverence for the private (Partners') office equal to that of the Greeks for the occupiers of Olympus. One day a clear whistled tune came to his ears. His head bobbed up above the screen of his loose-box, and with a scandalised voice he called out "Mr. Gillanders! How dare you!". However it was the senior partner, Robert, who guffawed and confessed that he was the culprit. It was the only time in five years that I ever saw Johnny Boadle taken aback. That a Partner, a Senior Partner, the successor of a line of dignified, white-whiskered, frock-coated Quaker William Rathbones, should light-heartedly whistle in the office! He hardly spoke a word for the rest of the day. He taught me much, especially discipline. – I owe much to the memory of Johnny Boadle…

'Mr. Ireland. Late thirties. Shipping clerk, responsible for all the bills of lading and other South American wool invoices and other documents. He had the neatest and most attractive writing of any I have known. He taught me how to work out an invoice for a wool consignment in Argentine dollars from the originals in Paraguayan dollars, and then into l.s.d., and the mysteries of dock dues and commission…

'From the 1st January each winter we sweated all-out to improve on the record date of achieving the annual balance. In those three years we got it down from three weeks to twelve days, by working till 9 pm sometimes, and finally, in the last year, we got our balance at 11 pm on the 12th January. On nights when we carded on beyond 6 pm we drew 1/6d tea money. I don't think the Partners ever knew how late we stayed, but we "achieved merit" among our fellow workers and were proud of it…

'In my last year I served as cashier and learned how to tell a genuine £5 note from a forgery at a glance. I was also responsible for bringing down from the Bank of Liverpool the two heavy tin boxes full of Bearer Bonds and cutting off the interest coupons on their due

William Rathbone VIII.

dates. We kept all the private accounts of all the Rathbone cousins, and Bearer Bonds, especially in U.S.A. securities, were popular in those days, which luckily for us were before the era of bank robberies and the street slugging of bank messengers.'

Despite the precautions that William took to strengthen the management of the firm – and because Robert's eccentricity often overcame his shrewdness – 'new' Rathbones got off to a rocky start. Within a year, the new partners had lost large amounts of money speculating in wool, and went on to compound their errors by trying to trade on the uncertainties created by the Boer War. Robert went out to Cape Town and opened an office to import mules, grain and wool from Argentina. Maybe he had heard that the firm always did well out of wars, but not this time. The business sputtered, and the office was soon closed. By 1905, Rathbones was once again in trouble. But William VI had died in 1902, and who was to sort it out now?

Wool being graded, 1900.

On William's death, his interest in the firm had passed to his youngest son Francis Warre Rathbone, known as Frank, who was 27 when he became a partner. However, Frank spent most of his time in Argentina where he was looking after family interests, and knew little of what was going on in Liverpool. When he finally returned to England in 1908, he found the firm in a disastrous condition. According to Lucie Nottingham's account of this period, the partners had piled up huge losses, with Robert Rathbone's personal share alone amounting to £20,000 because of what Hugh Rathbone described as his 'apparent inability to adhere to any line of policy previously agreed upon'. Once again, drastic action was called for. For the second time in only ten years, the disposal of the firm was considered – but rejected by Frank who resolved

Francis Warre Rathbone. 'Frank', William Rathbone VI's youngest son, joined Rathbones in 1902 and was a partner until his death in 1939.

to take it on himself, with appropriate arrangements to permit Robert and Arthur Radford to make a dignified exit. Hugh Rathbone was warm in his praise for Frank's courage and family loyalty. He wrote: 'It must be remembered that but for [Frank's] willingness to continue the business, this goodwill would have ceased altogether in so much as [Robert], being unable to go on by himself, it would have been put up for sale, and in the state of the firm at the end of 1908, without a Rathbone in the firm or any Rathbone connections it is hardly likely that the name of Rathbone Bros. & Co. would have any financial value.'

It took four more painful years to sort things out, but when the firm was finally restructured in 1912 with £20,000 in capital from the reserve fund, Hugh Rathbone wrote of the now departed Robert: 'He ought to have retired eight or nine years ago... I am satisfied that the firm can make money, and with the [Robert] incubus removed, I believe they will.' The way he saw it making money was by engineering a complete break from the merchanting business, and transforming itself into a finance house.

It is from this second restructuring that Rathbones' new existence as a financial services company should really be dated. One of the firm's first actions was to move out of the old merchant house in Water Street, where Rathbones had been since 1868, into spanking new premises in the recently completed Royal Liver Building, the grandest of the 'Three Graces' on the Liverpool waterfront. Unlike the cramped earlier quarters, the offices here were

Rathbones moved in 1912 to a prestigious office in the recently completed Royal Liver Building on the Mersey waterfront.

Rathbones was well positioned to offer financial services to wealthy clients as they had strong links with the commercial families of Liverpool. Shown here is Sudley House, a magnificent house owned by the Holt shipping family which is now a museum.

described as 'commodious and modern'.

Little documentation has survived to tell us how Frank and his colleagues devised their new business strategy. It could have simply evolved from the earlier course laid down by William VI to engage in 'the management of investments…'. Or it could have been a more deliberate attempt to exploit what the partners saw as a new business opportunity: providing a full investment management service for wealthy people who were too busy to watch their money closely or handle the paperwork and tax.

A brochure printed in 1912 strongly suggests that it was the latter. The range of services offered is wide, and charges are explicit. Under the heading CAPITAL MANAGEMENT, Rathbones 'undertake the supervision of investments', including the collection of dividends and interest, and the management of details such as rights issues. They also conduct periodic reviews of client portfolios and advise on purchase and sales of securities. In addition 'any special circumstances affecting their holdings are reported to clients as they occur, and advice is tendered as to the action to be taken'. All this is done for a charge of 1/8 per cent of the gross capital holdings. Among the other services offered by Rath-

bones are plain stockbroking, the management of trusts and estates, tax and insurance advice, cash accounts and the custody of securities. The firm even had its own investment trust, launched in 1911.

The brochure says: 'Clients will find that this system of management is not only economical but relieves them of much work and anxiety, especially in the case of Trusts and Settlements. Purchases and sales are only made on the written authority of clients, and in submitting suggestions, special attention is paid to individual circumstances and requirements.' This service is not far from that offered by Rathbones today.

Their market was potentially huge, and Frank and his partners would have known their prospective clients well. The Rathbones were close to all the big commercial families in Liverpool – by acquaintance, by marriage, through business connections – and they knew who was wealthy, who needed help running their finances, who was ambitious to build up capital. Liverpool in the Edwardian age was one of the richest cities in England, with family dynasties like the Bibbys, the Holts and the Pilkingtons amassing large fortunes. Although much of the grandeur of that age has now faded, it can still be glimpsed in the magnificence of the city's offices and municipal buildings, in the mansions facing on to Sefton Park, and in the grand country houses beyond the city boundaries and on the Wirral. These were houses designed for the grandest lifestyles, with banqueting halls, music rooms, picture galleries and palatial conservatories containing the latest botanic curiosities from all over the world. Perfect for the new Rathbones' business.

Although Frank was in charge, he was backed by Hugh Rathbone and Henry Gair Rathbone, his much older half-brother who came in a few days a week. But he needed extra support. Hugh Rathbone found it in the form of Vere Cotton, a young man whom he originally hired to tutor his sons in 1910. Hugh was so impressed by his energy and intelligence that he offered him a job at Rathbones with the promise that if things worked out he could become partner.

Cotton accepted. One of his earliest tasks was to write investment guides and provide clients with market summaries and advice – he was Rathbones' first 'financial analyst'. In reviewing the highly unsettled European scene in July 1914, he showed a

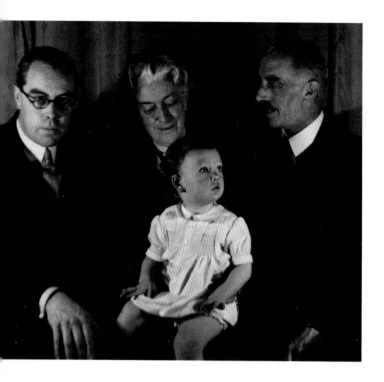

According to two private client ledgers which survive for the years 1932 to 1938 and have been studied by Lucie Nottingham, Rathbones was dealing on behalf of about 120 clients of whom more than 30 were members of the Rathbone family. The others included well-known Liverpool names such as the Mellys and the Moores. The services the firm performed for them were mainly investment management and family trusts. Each client was looked after on a very personal basis by a partner, more as a friend than a business associate, and enduring relationships were cemented, some lasting to this day.

By the 1930s, the memory of Rathbones as a merchant house was beginning to fade: they had not been in that line of business for a generation. Instead, the firm was acquiring a new reputation as a financial manager, associated with the best and wealthiest of Liverpool's business classes. Just before the Second World War, Evelyn Rathbone (a Rathbone through and through: she was Frank's sister and Hugh's wife) wrote that she and Hugh had placed all their money with Rathbones. 'They have benefited us all, and I have complete faith in the new firm. I believe they are going to be very cautious, reasonable and careful…'

When Frank died in 1939, the goodwill of the business passed to his son Bertram Lyle Rathbone, known as Larry, who had joined the firm in 1934 after completing his education at the London School of Economics. Like Cotton before him, he was immediately snatched away by war, leaving Cotton, as the new senior partner, to steer Rathbones through the difficult war years when the office and its historic contents were destroyed by bombs. This tragic event cost Rathbones not only its records but also priceless portraits and furniture – and forced it back into cramped quarters in Castle Street.

Once the war was over, Larry rejoined the firm, which was barely ticking over: in 1948, client cash balances were reported to be a mere £80,000. But Larry and Cotton set about rebuilding the business, literally from ruins. They were both military types, disciplined and undaunted, and they got to work with determination. These were not easy times for anyone in the wealth management business. Aside from the aftermath of war, the 1950s were a period of huge social change, of austerity, of nationalisation, of adjustment to the reality that Britain was no longer a world power, something that many Liver-

Four generations of Rathbones, from left, William Rathbone IX, Blanche, widow of William Rathbone VII with Bill Rathbone X on her lap, and William Rathbone VIII, 1937.

The German Luftwaffe (Air Force) carried out around 80 air raids on Merseyside between August 1940 and January 1942. The bombing was aimed mainly at the docks, railways and factories, but large areas were destroyed or damaged on both sides of the Mersey. Over 4,000 people died. The Rathbones' office was badly bombed and they relocated to Castle Street.

good grasp of ominous events. 'The situation in Albania is still full of grave difficulties, but the latest reports indicate that Prince William is achieving some success against the rebels. Unfortunately, any gain in this quarter of South-east Europe has been completely discounted by the terrible tragedy at Serajevo [sic] where the murder of the Austrian heir and his wife indicates how deep-rooted is the hatred of Austrian Rule, and how thin is the veneer which annexation has spread over the turbulent Serbs of Bosnia and Herzegovina. The assassination still further complicates the political situation which is bound to arise in the regrettable event of the death of the present Emperor of Austria.' Cotton went on to recommend several stocks in the Americas, presumably fearing the worst.

Inconveniently, these very same events took Cotton away from Rathbones and into the army. But he survived the First World War and returned to Liverpool in 1919 to take up his promised partnership. It was the start of an impressive career with the firm that was to last until 1960 and make him the pillar of the business. With his military bearing and ever-present pipe, he was always known as The Colonel.

Unfortunately the records for the inter-war period were either destroyed or remain under lock and key for reasons of client confidentiality, so it is hard to say how large or profitable the business became.

Vere Cotton as Lord Mayor of Liverpool, 1951.

pudlians found hard to believe. Liverpool itself was heading into steep decline as the port business moved elsewhere, with little to replace it. Many Rathbones clients saw their fortunes melt away or decided to leave. But Larry and Cotton stuck by the city. Cotton joined the city council and rose to become Lord Mayor in 1951; he was also active on the council of Liverpool University and played a leading role in the long-running campaign to finish the city's Anglican cathedral. Larry became treasurer of the university and continued Rathbones' tradition of local philanthropy.

As post-war normality returned, their steadfastness began to pay off. By 1959 cash balances had reached £188,000, by which time the firm had about 500 clients, a sharp improvement on pre-war numbers. Larry's philosophy was to hold on to existing clients by offering them a highly personalised service, and only accept new ones on personal recommendation so that a bond existed from the start. This created a sense of loyalty between the firm and its clients in a period when economic pressures and new marketing techniques were beginning to erode financial relationships. It is said of Larry that one way he kept balances up was by refusing to let female clients withdraw any money. This may not be

true, but this was still an age when women were not thought capable of understanding finance. Most of Rathbones' profits around this time came from a turn on stock exchange commissions and interest on client balances rather than management fees.

When Cotton retired in 1960, Larry took over as senior partner, and continued to run Rathbones on strict military lines, doing things his way with little time for other people's. Mary Armitage, who joined the firm as a copy typist in 1968, recalls him being kindly but firm. 'His word was the law!' He addressed women as Mrs or Miss, and men by their surnames. The firm was still small, a staff of a dozen people in two rooms who ran the customer accounts using pen, paper and mental arithmetic, and entered them into huge ledgers which the female members found impossible to lift – though they had to be locked away in the stockroom safe each night. There were still relics of the Edwardian age: tall leather-topped desks, armchairs, a strong sense of propriety, and lack of urgency. Paul Loughlin, who joined as postroom boy in 1983, had the job of wheeling around heavy metal trolleys containing punch card files, and running through the city streets hand-delivering messages to brokers and clients. Both Armitage and Loughlin are still with

© Imperial War Museum D5983

the firm in 2008, a sign of its enduring values.

The low profile adopted by Rathbones was very much in keeping with the Rathbones tradition and Larry's preferences. It also added a dash of mystique to the firm. Roy Morris, who joined as a bookkeeper in 1957, recalls that there were 19 stockbrokers in Liverpool at the time, and Rathbones was a bit of a mystery to all of them. No one was quite sure what they did, who their clients were, how they earned their keep. This was understandable: stockbrokers dominated the scene, but Rathbones was content to look after people's money and leave the broking to others. Larry did try new ventures: investment trusts and a joint venture with Keyser Ullman, the City merchant bank, as a way into corporate business, though this ended when the latter folded in 1976.

As the firm grew, Larry took on new partners. One was a new Rathbone: Sebastian, a grandson of Hugh Rathbone who joined in 1960. Sebastian was a man of exceptional gifts: he was a Cambridge maths scholar, an accomplished skier and a hockey blue. Deciding to become an accountant, he came second in the national accountancy exams. But much of this was hidden behind a modest manner that found favour with colleagues and clients. He also brought to the firm a fascination with computers which was to become a catalyst for change at a key moment in its evolution.

Larry also decided to cast his net wider. Through the Cambridge University Appointments Board he found John Leigh, who had been working as a

Larry Rathbone.

The retirement party for Vere Cotton (standing sixth from right) in 1960. Larry Rathbone, his successor as senior partner is to Vere's right. Sebastian Rathbone is on the extreme left.

Sebastian Rathbone.

Rathbone partners, 1991. From left, John Leigh, Roy Morris, Sebastian Rathbone, Anthony Nottingham and Anthony Furse.

merchant in West Africa; he joined the firm in 1963. Sebastian also put forward Anthony Furse, a fellow chartered accountant who was company secretary of Cammell Laird in Birkenhead. Furse joined in 1970 and became a partner a year later, initially to oversee the Keyser Ullman link, and later to manage funds.

The partners occupied a separate room the other side of the corridor where they handled the client relationships and investment decisions. They each 'owned' their clients, often personal friends. The style of the business was very much one of partnership: the partners' money financed the firm, and they shared out the profits. If you asked a partner for a pay rise, you felt the money was coming straight out of his own pocket. John Leigh recalls that the slump in the stock market in the mid-1970s left the partners 'frightfully bankrupt, but we got through that and it picked up again'.

Under Sebastian, part of the new partners' job was to persuade Larry to modernise the business, and several steps were taken to 'upgrade' the firm.

Since Rathbones handled a lot of client cash, it made sense to have a banking licence. When the Bank of England set up a new register of Licensed Deposit Takers in the early 1970s after the secondary banking crisis, Rathbones applied. John Leigh went down to London to be vetted by the Bank. An official asked him how long Rathbones had been in business, since the Bank did not issue licences to fly-by-nights. Leigh pointed out that Rathbones had been around almost as long as the Bank, and had moreover supplied it with a Governor. The licence came through without a hitch, but the capital requirements for banking status were onerous for a partnership, and this led to a decision to incorporate the business in the late 1970s, though as an unlimited company to underline the partners' commitment.

The late 1970s also saw a period of technological change. It was clear that the punched card system on which the firm depended needed to be replaced with something electronic: it took a clerk two weeks to draw up clients' quarterly bank statements, and the bookkeepers four months to complete the annual accounts. Sebastian was keen that the firm obtain the latest technology rather than something too cautious. Furse was given the task of coming up with proposals. Although IBM seemed the natural choice, he ended up recommending a British-made system that was a fraction of the price. Sebastian persuaded a reluctant Larry to invest in it; the system proved a success and reduced the bookkeeping tasks to a matter of hours.

By the time Larry retired in 1982, Rathbones was managing about £75m of other people's money, a considerable achievement given his meagre inheritance after the war. But his personality remained deeply stamped on the business. Brian Kenny, who joined in 1981 as a graduate recruit, found it 'a rather formal environment, though moving gradually into more relaxed times. It was sleepy but not a backwater. They were very good at what they did. Very international. Rathbones have always been very outward-looking.'

Larry was succeeded by Sebastian who continued to push for modernisation in his low-key way. Budgeting, cost management, streamlining became part of the day-to-day workings of the growing business. An important change was the introduction of nominee accounts. Under this arrangement the fund manager holds the shares on behalf of the client, making it much easier – and cheaper – for him to run the account and initiate transactions.

Over this period, Roy Morris began to emerge as a new force in the firm. Energetic, good with people, keen to introduce new practices, he became an assistant partner in 1978 and a full partner in 1983. Now with four partners, a growing business and a staff of 70 people, Rathbones had outgrown its Castle Street premises, and decided on a move back to the Three Graces. This time it was the top floor of the magnificent Port of Liverpool Building, with fine views over the docks and river from which the firm had sprung two and a half centuries before.

By the 1980s, the whole of Rathbones' business environment was changing. The arrival of the Thatcher era with Big Bang (see box on page 119) and privatisation of nationalised industries gave a huge boost to the equity markets and to the number of private investors. It also unleashed a great wave of consolidation in the City of London. Banks began to buy up stockbrokers (including Tilney, Liverpool's largest), and foreign competitors poured into the market. Being small and special no longer seemed a prudent strategy in the face of such momentous developments. Not for the first time, Rathbones had to consider its future.

Famous Rathbones

Eleanor Rathbone.

Eleanor Rathbone MP, William VI's second daughter, was a leading social campaigner, fighting for women's rights and better conditions for the poor. Born in 1872, she studied at Oxford University and joined her father in the closing years of his life in compiling a major report on the tough working conditions of Liverpool dockers. After he died, she helped set up the School of Social

A cartoon from 1930 showing Eleanor Rathbone (holding the crocodile) fighting for family allowances. In 1945, a year before her death, the Family Allowance Act was finally passed.

Science at Liverpool University, and became an independent member of Liverpool City Council, the start of a political career which led to her becoming, in 1929, one of the country's first woman MPs. A relation described her as 'awfully sane, with hard red cheeks'. Alongside her fight for human rights, Eleanor embraced many specific causes: family allowances paid directly to mothers, the condition of indigenous women in British colonies, the families of soldiers killed or wounded in the First World War, and benefits for families of the unemployed. She also wrote a biography of her father. In the 1930s she was an early member of the anti-Nazi movement, and in 1938 denounced the Munich Agreement. She never married. After her death in 1946, a charitable trust was created in her name to pursue her causes.

Kirkdale election campaign in Liverpool 1910. Eleanor Rathbone is second from the left.

Basil Rathbone, the actor famed worldwide for his portrayal of Sherlock Holmes, was a cousin of the main Rathbone line. He was born in Johannesburg in 1892 where his father Edgar was a mining engineer. The family had to flee the country during the Boer War, and Basil was brought up in England where he soon decided that he wanted to go on the stage. He got started through a cousin who ran a theatre company, and after breaking off to serve in the First World War, went to New York to try his luck on Broadway. With his darkly handsome looks he won parts as the suave villain, and eventually caught the eye of Hollywood, where he went to live in the 1930s. Here he made his first Sherlock Holmes film, *The Hound of the Baskervilles*, in 1939, which was a great success and led to a dozen more plus a string of radio shows. He became one of the most widely recognised faces in film. But Basil tired of the typecasting, and returned to the stage in New York where he ran a one-man show and did the occasional play and film. He died there in 1967 aged 75.

Basil Rathbone.

THESE SEE THE WORKS

OF THE LORD

Rathbones' Liverpool office is in the Port of Liverpool Building which was built as the head office of the Mersey Docks and Harbour Board and opened in 1907. The frieze, in the magnificent entrance hall quotes the Bible, Psalm 107: 'They that go down to the sea in ships that do business in great waters these see the works of the Lord and his wonders of the deep.'

The fall and rise of Liverpool

The year 1907 was a magnificent time to be alive in Liverpool. The second greatest port in the Empire was 700 years old, and revelling in its glory. There were celebrations, pageants, brass bands and banquets. Huge symbolic projects were in hand: a new university, a new cathedral and the new Port of Liverpool Building, the first of the 'Three Graces' that were to adorn the waterfront. The previous year, the city had even scored a football double: Liverpool FC became league champions and Everton won the FA Cup.

St George's Plateau, at the heart of the city, contained some of England's finest municipal buildings including St George's Hall, modelled on the Parthenon in Athens. Wealth spilled out of Liverpool's elegant Georgian terraces and grand suburban mansions. The busy docks stretched for miles along the riverfront, handling goods from all over the world. Transatlantic passengers streamed through its terminals, the rich with their servants, the poor seeking a new life across the water. All these had helped earn Liverpool its status as a 'city' in 1880.

It was hard to imagine that it could possibly end. But even as the celebrations began, the signs of imminent decline were to be seen. In the spring of 1907, the White Star Line, the biggest passenger ship company operating out of Merseyside, decided to transfer its operations from Liverpool to Southampton to be nearer London and the French ports. Although Halifax-based Cunard later set up its European headquarters in Liverpool, passenger numbers never recovered. Cargo shippers moved to London and Bristol for

Statue of Edward VII by the Port of Liverpool Building.

The Three Graces with the newly-restored Albert Dock on the left.

similar reasons. Within only four years of the anniversary, the whole of Liverpool docks was brought to a standstill by striking dockers, desperate for work.

The city itself was also fighting a losing battle against the legacy of commercial success: massive overcrowding, homelessness and disease, much of it resulting from the 19th-century immigration from Ireland. Despite having appointed Britain's first medical officer of health (in 1847), and launched one of the country's first council housing projects (in the 1860s), most of the city's residents lived in unrelieved squalor. And these problems intensified as Liverpool's prosperity waned and the municipal budget shrank.

Within 20 years of the anniversary, Liverpool was in steep decline. Many of the docks were idle, hit by changing patterns of trade and the collapse of the industries of the North West, particularly textiles. Two world wars and a depression added to the pain. In the 1930s the population began to shrink from its peak of around 950,000, and eventually reached half that size, a dreadful blow to its pride and its economy. Beatlemania and other bursts of local enthusiasm like the 1984 International Garden Festival gave the city an occasional lift but could not stem the fall which reached its nadir in 1993 when Liverpool was given Objective One status, the European Union's top measure of urban deprivation.

But it was a nadir. Although Liverpool had earned itself a reputation for self-pity, it found a new determination to get back on its feet. Aided by regional grants and morale-boosting projects like the restoration of the Albert Dock, the recovery began. Fresh investment arrived, new businesses opened. Even the docks re-engineered themselves

Small Concert Room, St George's Hall.

for the container age: today they handle more tonnage than ever before, though with a fraction of the manpower.

In 2008, Liverpool's recovery was crowned with the title 'European Capital of Culture', an award which not only did wonders for the city's self-esteem but gave recognition to the richness of a history and cultural attainment which had been obscured by the grime and deprivation of too many bad years. The award also gave Liverpool a reason to spruce itself up, to restore its neglected streets, clean up the waterfront and encourage exciting new developments, like the Paradise Project, a 42-acre city centre regeneration scheme, the largest in Europe.

There is still a long way to go: whole areas of the city are still awaiting new investment, and the shape of the new economy has yet to establish itself. But for the first time in 100 years, Liverpudlians are reading good news rather than bad.

7

THE NEW RATHBONES
1988–2008

Around the time Rathbones moved into the Port of Liverpool building in 1984, a new company was floated on the Unlisted Securities Market (USM), the junior arm of the London Stock Exchange. It had the inelegant

UNIVERSITY HOUSE

A painting by David
Gentleman of Rathbones'
London office at Lower
Grosvenor Place, Victoria,
1985.

CFS directors before the merger with Rathbones. Left to right, Micky Ingall, Ian Harvey, Michael Bryant, Oliver Stanley, Colin Kinloch and John Tuck.

CFS was the brainchild of a former barrister and tax inspector called Oliver Stanley. Liverpool-born, Stanley was an ambitious and non-conformist type: he enjoyed challenging the established order and took pleasure in being different. Under wartime university arrangements, he was allocated a place at Christ Church, Oxford, where he became an expert on the works of Henry James and almost took up an academic career. But after pursuing this interest at Harvard he came back to England and, on a whim, answered a job advertisement for the Inland Revenue. He spent ten years there; on one occasion he met James Callaghan, the Chancellor of the Exchequer, and offered him some unsought advice. Callaghan fobbed him off, which Stanley enjoyed. But eventually the same tax files started coming round again, and Stanley needed to move on. He read for the Bar, but ended up joining Inchcape, the trading conglomerate, as a tax consultant in the early 1970s.

Inchcape had a variety of financial interests including banking and insurance, and Stanley could see that many of its personal clients would welcome a one-stop shop that could manage their tax and financial affairs. This was a time when Denis Healey, the new Chancellor of the Exchequer, was threatening to squeeze the rich until 'the pips squeaked'. Inchcape thought it was a good idea and teamed up with Pearson, the owner of Lazard and the *Financial Times*, to create the new company with Stanley as its managing director, with a ten per cent interest. The philosophy behind CFS was quite new at the time. Stockbrokers, accountants and fund managers had always offered their services separately. To have them all together was extremely convenient, and Stanley and his colleagues Colin Kinloch and John Keeton soon found themselves 'whizzing up and down the country, visiting people in their castles and stately homes, and on their islands, explaining the rules of estate duty, setting up trusts'.

By 1974, Inchcape and Pearson had developed other interests and agreed to sell the company to Stanley and his colleagues for £10,000. They moved into new premises in Cockspur Street off Trafalgar Square which was handy for gentlemen visiting their clubs in nearby St James's. Stanley forged a link with the Country Landowners Association which brought in new clients, and with every new tax that Healey introduced, CFS's business swelled. But these good years came to an end when Mrs Thatcher won the general election in 1979 and set about cutting taxes. The time had come for CFS to alter course: instead of protecting wealth, the future lay in generating it.

Stanley was ambitious for CFS but lacked the cash to acquire new businesses. This led to the decision to float the company so that he could use its shares as currency to buy other firms. When CFS obtained its listing in September 1984, it had a market value of £2.8m with profits forecast for that year of £250,000. The first deal Stanley did was with two City men who managed funds and were looking for a partner to grow with, Micky Ingall and Jonathan Ruffer who were both at Allied Dunbar at the time.

This was a period when most wealthy people in Britain still kept their money with a stockbroker, who earned his living by advising them and taking commissions on stock exchange deals. But many large City firms had difficulty making their private client business pay: it was labour-intensive and costly, and often amounted to little more than 'stick 'em into BP and take 'em out to lunch'. Ingall and Ruffer viewed the scene differently. They saw a business in which wealthy people would give their money to professional managers to look after on a discretionary basis for a fee linked to the capital sum. This was much more efficient because the fund manager had complete administrative and investment control over the account, with a steadier revenue flow. The challenge was to get clients to understand the approach, and agree to sign their assets over to the manager.

Stanley could see the possibilities of the model. He, Ingall and Ruffer agreed to join forces using a pricing formula that would become standard in CFS's future growth: two per cent of the value of funds brought in. It was an excellent match which brought CFS £35m of new funds under management, and gave Ingall and Ruffer ten per cent of CFS each. Investment management soon became the dominant part of CFS's business, with funds rapidly moving up to £100m. So what next?

In early 1987, Ingall received a phone call from Anthony Nottingham, a stockbroking friend who was now a partner at Rathbones in Liverpool. Ingall had heard of Rathbones but, like many people in the business, was not sure exactly what they did. Nottingham replied: 'The same as you, only they don't make much money at it.' Ingall had also heard that Rathbones was a very dynastic firm that kept its doors tightly shut against would-be acquirers.

But times were changing at Rathbones as well. The new blood injected by Roy Morris and other newcomers was making it more ambitious for growth and profits, and the partners knew that it needed to become much bigger if it was to match the heavy guns that were emerging in the wake of Big Bang. But with Liverpool now in decline, it was difficult to attract human and financial capital. The Liverpool stock exchange, once the heart of the business community, had been rolled up with Manchester and other regional exchanges into the Northern Exchange in the 1960s, and then closed in the 1970s. The number of local stockbrokers and fund managers had shrunk to a mere handful. Acquisition or merger were therefore becoming serious propositions for Rathbones. Futhermore, Sebastian understood the choices and was more open to propositions than his predecessors: he had even met Ingall at various City occasions and on the ski slopes of Klosters.

Nottingham arranged a meeting in Liverpool.

The date turned out to be unpropitious: two days after the big market crash in October 1987, but at least that meant people would have to be realistic about prices. Ingall travelled up by train and was shown into a boardroom with generations of Rathbone portraits staring down at him. There, he met the partners who were hospitable but, it seemed to him, wary. The documentation he was given showed that they had about £200m under management, which was impressive, but were earning profits of only £0.5m in a good year, which was well under par by City standards. When Ingall asked to see a sales brochure, he was told that they had all been used up, but someone might be able to provide a photocopy. When the document arrived Ingall noticed that it was dated 1912.

But this inauspicious start did not stall the negotiations. It was plain to Ingall that Rathbones had huge potential: its client base was top class, and its inefficiencies could be viewed as scope to improve earnings, especially since Rathbones had the same computer system as CFS. Moreover, it soon became clear that the main obstacle to a deal was one that Ingall could easily remove: the name. Sebastian was proposing to end more than 250 years of independence, but he wanted to preserve the Rathbone name. Ingall had long wanted to drop the name of Comprehensive Financial Services (it had come to be known in the firm as Curiously Friendly Services) so to exchange it for one with centuries of tradition was nothing but a bonus. Rathbone Bros. & Co. it would be.

Larry, in retirement, let it be known that he opposed the deal, but the existing partners all came round to it in the end. Looking back on the outcome, Leigh says: 'It was necessary. I don't think we could have continued on our own,' and Anthony Furse agrees, 'The merger was right for the firm: a very sensible solution.'

The deal was struck on the now established lines. The Rathbones partners would get two per cent of the funds they delivered to CFS, provided the clients signed a new management agreement with CFS, banked with them and agreed to have their stock held in nominee accounts. Sebastian wrote them a nice letter, and every single one of them came. The partners ended up with 35 per cent of the enlarged company in a deal which gave the combined business a value of £12m, and enabled CFS to triple its

Big Bang – dramatic change

Mrs Thatcher, the architect of Big Bang, 1986.

In 1986, Rathbones' investment business was transformed by an event which came to be known as Big Bang. This was the reform of the London Stock Exchange imposed by Mrs Thatcher in her drive to make the City more open and competitive.

Before that date, the Stock Exchange was a self-regulated club to which only British individuals could belong. It was also a monopoly which controlled all dealing in UK stocks and fixed the commissions that investors had to pay.

Following Mrs Thatcher's threat to bring a monopoly charge, the Exchange agreed to get rid of these restrictions and open itself up to all-comers. The event was called Big Bang because it all happened at once, on October 27th 1986, rather than in stages.

The effect was swift and dramatic. Banks quickly took advantage by buying up Stock Exchange firms, and turning themselves into huge financial conglomerates offering cut-price services to win business.

Although the aftermath of Big Bang was bloody – many banks lost large amounts of money – it altered the character of the City for good by ending the days of small private firms and putting a premium on size and competitiveness. It was against this background that Rathbones had to consider its future as a small regional partnership.

The London Stock Exchange on the day of Big Bang, 1986.

funds under management in exchange for only half of its equity. For the partners it was a handsome reward for steering the family firm into a safe berth.

It was, of course, a takeover by CFS. For reasons of tact, family feelings, continuity and the preservation of the name, it was presented as a merger of equals. Sebastian became deputy chairman to Stanley, Ingall was chief executive, and Morris was put in charge of the Liverpool office. Other executives included Ian Harvey, the finance director, and Michael Bryant, the marketing director. Although the headquarters shifted to London, it was decided that alternate board meetings should be held in Liverpool to give the office an added sense of involvement.

Nonetheless, news of the merger sent shivers through Merseyside's 60-strong staff where the immediate fear was that jobs would be moved to London. In fact, the opposite happened: back-office jobs were transferred from London's high-cost environment to Liverpool, which eventually became the centre of operations for the whole business with greatly expanded office space. The promotion of Morris, a Liverpudlian born and bred, was also reassuring. Mary Armitage, who by now had been with the firm 20 years, believes that 'we drew the long straw', though her main memories of the merger are of the frenzy that followed as back-office systems were combined.

The Rathbones that emerged from the merger, consummated in 1988, was a firm nearly double the size, with a new corporate culture, a stock market quotation, large offices in Liverpool and London, and ambitions to keep growing. Internally, there was a drive for efficiency, even the introduction of business targets which some of the older hands found unfamiliar. Brian Kenny, who had joined seven years previously, welcomed developments: 'It was a great opportunity. Change was gradual because the people remained the same, but the potential opened up dramatically. We saw the emergence of a corporate mentality. The introduction of share options created a reward structure which opened up a more diverse ownership. It was quite different from the relationship we had before.'

Sebastian and his partners stayed on to see the merger through, but retired soon afterwards, leaving the firm in the hands of a contrasting trio: Oliver Stanley, the contrarian, Micky Ingall, the polished

Etonian, and Roy Morris, the bustling Liverpudlian. But it worked. They shared a vision: to build on Rathbones' name for quality and CFS's business skills to grow the firm into a leading force in private client wealth management. In order to create a sense of continuity, and to reassure clients and staff, Ingall invited William Rathbone X, the great-great-grandson of William VI, to join the board where he stayed for nine years, becoming senior non-executive director.

The CFS/Rathbones merger ushered in a period of expansion that lasted, unbroken, up to the new century as Rathbones beefed up its management and went on the acquisition trail for more business. The key was to be selective, to find people and firms who fitted the special Rathbones culture. Ingall talked of 'finding like souls in other places'. According to Stanley, the priority was to be prudent, not to upset the firm's affairs or client relationships, but to proceed as and when the opportunity arose. Caution was certainly justified. Clients in the wealth management business view their relationships as being with their investment managers rather than the firm, and this can cut both ways. If disaffected investment managers leave, they take their clients with them. But if they can be wooed over from other firms, they bring their clients with them too. Among the first to come, in 1990, were an investment team from Sheppards, the London stockbrokers, and the next year the Leather brothers, Michael and Mark, joined from Ashton Tod McLaren, a Liverpool rival. As before, Rathbones paid two per cent for funds brought by the new arrivals.

By the early 1990s, growth was acquiring a strong momentum, and the time had come to move Rathbones up from the USM to a full listing on the London Stock Exchange. This happened in June 1992 with an introduction document which forecast group profits for that year of £4m, more than double the £1.5m earned in the first year after the merger. Funds under management were now on the brink of the £1bn mark, and staff numbers stood at 124. The reason for the float was given as the need for 'enhanced status and a wider investment profile' – in other words to tap a bigger shareholder base. It was a good moment to float: April had seen the surprise re-election of a Conservative government, and the markets were gearing up for five more glorious years.

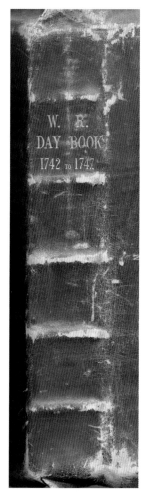

The spine of the Day Book from 1742–1747.

Roy Morris and Oliver Stanley chat to Eddie George, the Governor of the Bank of England, at the opening of the New Bond Street office in 1997.

The year 1992 was memorable for another reason: it marked the 250th anniversary of the Day Book started by William Rathbone II back in 1742, and it called for a celebration. Rathbones threw a party in the Bank of England Museum at which one of the speakers was Peter Baring, chairman of Barings, who joked that he would not be there but for Lidderdale rescuing his bank more than 100 years before. Shortly afterwards, history was to repeat itself for Barings, but this time with fatal results.

The float reinforced Rathbones' successful strategy by giving wider currency to its shares as a means of financing growth, and further acquisitions quickly followed. One was of a group of fund managers from Framlington Investment Management, which provoked a legal blocking action by Framlington. The team succeeded in coming, but Rathbones had to settle with Framlington and take on board the message that 'poaching' required a certain caution.

By 1995 Rathbones had developed the appetite for a larger acquisition, particularly one which would establish it as a firm of substance rather than one with a string of smaller interests. One prospect was Laurence Keen, a well-established City stock-broker and fund manager which, like many such firms in the aftermath of Big Bang, had undergone several changes of ownership and needed a more settled partner. Ingall initiated discussions with Bill Keatley, the chairman, and proposed the customary formula of two per cent of discretionary funds, with two years to complete the conversion of clients. To speed things up, Ingall said he would make an initial payment of £10m, with the total capped at £25m in order to comply with the Stock Exchange's listing rules. This sum seemed considerably more than the final bill was likely to be, but Laurence Keen clients came in large numbers, and the final calculation came out at £26m, meaning that Rathbones actually saved £1m on the price.

The Laurence Keen merger was a big step forward, bringing Rathbones over £1bn of new funds. But Laurence Keen was truly a City firm, and its management was reluctant to leave its offices in Bow Lane for Rathbones' Victoria headquarters. Investment management did not happen in the West End, they said. There was a bit of a stand-off which was only resolved a year later when Rathbones and Laurence Keen both moved into 159 New Bond Street, in the heart of Mayfair. Eddie George, the Governor

In 1997 Rathbones moved from Victoria to prestigious premises in New Bond Street in the heart of Mayfair.

of the Bank of England, snipped the ribbon. The move proved a great success. Apart from providing much better accommodation for both firms, it showed that private clients actually preferred to visit their investment managers in Bond Street rather than on Cheapside, underlining in geographical terms the emergence of private wealth management as a business quite distinct from City stockbroking, which Rathbones was definitely not.

The chief executive of Laurence Keen was Mark Powell, a man of considerable City experience in fund management and broking who had previously run the private client business of Laing & Cruickshank, another well-established City firm. The acquisition raised the question of how to structure the merged management since there was already a chairman (Stanley) and a chief executive (Ingall). This was resolved by appointing Powell as joint managing director (alongside Morris), with responsibility for investment management. Two years later, in 1997, Stanley retired, at which point Ingall moved up to replace him, Morris became chief executive, and Powell became deputy chairman.

The success of the Laurence Keen acquisition left Rathbones eager for more, and the following year it made an offer to Neilson Cobbold, another Liverpool stockbroker, which was accepted on the

ROY MORRIS   MICKY INGALL   MARK POWELL   MARK PEARSON

The Rathbone Brothers Plc
Board in the late 1990s.

customary terms. Though smaller than Laurence Keen, Neilson Cobbold brought a different benefit: a network of regional offices which gave Rathbones a stronger presence in the South of England and in Edinburgh, both providing gateways to 'old money'. The Edinburgh business was later merged with two smaller acquisitions, and grew quickly under its new manager, John Henderson, to reach £1bn in assets. Two of Neilson Cobbold's directors joined the board – Mark Pearson in Liverpool and James Lifford, who was responsible for all of the Neilson Cobbold's other offices and was based in Winchester.

In the succeeding years, further teams came from a roll call of top financial institutions: Gerrard, Close Brothers, Dresdner Kleinwort Benson, Robert Fleming, HSBC, Schroders. On the trust side, which was the early driver of the CFS business, Rathbones acquired a clutch of Jersey-based firms to add to the presence it already had in Geneva and the British Virgin Islands, and was subsequently to have in Singapore as well. Though now overtaken by other activities in the firm, the trust business today provides an additional – and different – revenue flow to the firm's central wealth management activity, as well as a further service to attract and retain clients.

This rapid growth saw Rathbones absorbing

dozens of new people a year and adding billions to client assets, but it posed quite a management challenge.

Although much had been done in the 1990s by the Stanley/Ingall/Morris trio to raise efficiency and instil a more business-like spirit, Rathbones still retained something of the partnership culture about it. Until the Laurence Keen acquisition, it was run by people who had their roots in the original firms but lacked broader corporate experience. When William Rathbone X joined the board in 1994 he found what was essentially 'two unamalgamated partnerships'. Mark Powell's first impression on arriving from Laurence Keen was of people who did their own thing, of a governance structure that was rather clubbish, and technical support which seemed to be 'held together with sticky tape'. With its growing size and complexity, Rathbones needed a more solidly based corporate approach, though one which did not kill off the intangible qualities – the personal touch, the tradition – inherited from partnership days. The Laurence Keen and Neilson Cobbold acquisitions provided the catalyst by forcing Rathbones to raise its game. This was partly because the ownership of these firms took Rathbones into the stockbroking business where it became regulated by the Securities and Futures Authority (SFA), who demanded disciplined operating and management systems. But it was also internally generated: management, audit, the quality of the board, remuneration – all needed to be tightened up and brought in line with 'best practice'.

An early recruit was Andy Pomfret, a chartered accountant from Dresdner Kleinwort Benson who joined as finance director in 1999, the firm's first top professional appointment. Pomfret was not keen when approached for the job: he shared the popular view in the City of Rathbones as sleepy and backward. But that also made it a challenge. He came and embarked on 'professionalising' the firm, bringing in more qualified individuals like himself, upgrading internal reporting systems and opening up closer investor relations with the City. 'It was all part of progressing from a cosy partnership to a public company.'

Giving Rathbones a modern and robust operating system was another top priority. The task was assigned to Paul Chavasse, who joined the firm in 2001 from NatWest and Coutts. He found 'an excellent bedrock system' but one that needed 'a more grown-up management structure on top of it'. Over the next two years, Chavasse pulled the management and information systems together into a new nerve centre in Liverpool, streamlining Rathbones' internal operations and squeezing a lot of cost out of them as well. The new systems not only had to be able to handle an array of new investment instruments, such

as structured products and hedge funds, but also the torrent of regulation that was coming out of the newly created Financial Services Authority and Brussels. 'We're intrinsically reliant on IT systems', says Chavasse, who became chief operating officer. 'They are incredibly complicated. Only one per cent of the staff truly understand how they all interrelate. For the rest it's like a car, no one knows or investigates what goes on under the bonnet.'

Rathbones' greater professionalism also helped it to recruit new people. There was still much puzzlement in the City as to what Rathbones was (a company or a partnership?) and what it did (stockbroking, investment management?). Potential City recruits expected it to be eccentric and stuffy, which is how it seemed when they turned up for interview at a Bond Street address and found a reception area furnished with sofas and oil paintings of tea clippers. Rupert Baron, who joined from Gerrard in 2000, found it initially 'slightly Jurassic, technologically backward'. But like others before and after him, he came to view Rathbones as a free-standing company with an enterprising culture and an eagerness to do business. Andrew Hutton, who came with a self-contained team of five in 2001 from Flemings, had never heard of Rathbones 'but it turned out to be exactly what I was looking for: an independent private client house not owned by a large US bank trying to expand the business in huge leaps'.

Rathbones didn't pay top dollar, but it made up

Past and present chairmen, Oliver Stanley, Micky Ingall and Mark Powell.

for it in other ways. Richard Lanyon, who was one of the first to join in 1992 in the acrimonious split with Framlington, took a salary cut to come over because he 'wanted to move to an organisation which had made a commercial success of managing private client portfolios'. But by bringing £180m of funds, he and his two colleagues received nearly five per cent of the business at the time. Lanyon now runs the investment management side of Rathbones. 'People come here and stay because this is a business which takes an interest in them and their clients.'

Nonetheless, remuneration is crucial. Oliver Stanley was always a believer in incentive schemes, and his beliefs live on in a remuneration structure that is linked closely to results. A portion of the reward to staff is paid in shares in the company, and Ingall was gratified to see in 2002 that several dozen people owned shares worth more than £1m. Apart from spurring people to greater effort, this has given Rathbones a degree of protection against predators: more than 20 per cent of the shares are still owned by staff and other 'friendly hands'.

A particular appeal to individualists, which is what investment managers are, is the way Rathbones structures its investment management operation. Today, Rathbones has over 30,000 clients spread across the country, though skewed towards the South East. The typical client is over 55 with more than half a million pounds in liquid assets,

The annual Rathbones ski trip, 2006.

A team from Rathbones competed in Race for Life in 2007 to raise money for Cancer Research UK in support of Sue Desborough, finance director, who sadly passed away in November 2007.

Rathbones has over 30,000 clients. Fostering good client relations is at the core of the business.

and keen to conserve value; the typical relationship includes several members of the family spanning as many as four generations. This gives the business a solid, if conservative, character. Unlike many investment management firms where responsibilities are split between the people who make the investment decisions and those who manage relations with clients, Rathbones combines the two: the manager looks after the client, and decides on the most appropriate investments – which he or she is best placed to do. Overall investment guidance is provided by an Asset Allocation Committee consisting of section leaders who offer views about trends and investments. All client portfolios are closely monitored and linked to benchmarks so that management can quickly spot unusual movements and seek an explanation from the investment manager involved. Ian Buckley, a chartered accountant who joined the board as a non-executive director in 2001 and two years later became an executive running the trust business, says: 'It gives you freedom within a serious framework.'

Having sorted out management, Rathbones also had to look at its business spread. In the late 1990s, the question came up of whether it should establish itself in the unit trust business. It was one of those seminal moments which determine the character of a firm. Earlier acquisitions had brought several unit trusts with them, and this was clearly the direction in which the private investor market was heading: unit trusts were springing up like mushrooms. But unit trusts – managed funds of which investors can buy slices or units – are a 'product' as opposed to a service, and some of the Rathbones board felt this was not appropriate. Moreover, the performance of unit trusts is exposed to the public gaze. All a bit new. The first time the proposal came up before the board, it was rejected. But it was revived a couple of years later and went through on a nod. In 1999 Rathbones hired Peter Pearson Lund, one of the top people in the business who had previously run Gartmore and Henderson unit trusts. It was an excellent move: under Pearson Lund by 2007 unit trust funds under management had grown to £2bn, making

The executive committee, 2008. From left, Andy Pomfret, Richard Lanyon, Ian Buckley, Richard Loader and Paul Chavasse.

them an important contributor to profit, and greatly raising Rathbones' profile in the private investor market.

A more recent innovation is the introduction of 'alternatives', a euphemism for unconventional investments such as derivative-based products and hedge funds – a further test of Rathbones' ability to combine the traditional with the new. Rathbones needed to be sure that it could appraise these emerging opportunities and select the best for its clients. Hugh Adlington, a fund manager who joined from JP Morgan Fleming in 2001, took responsibility for researching them, and Rathbones now has an Alternative Assets Committee which does due diligence on an increasing flow of new issuance. But alternatives are not obvious investments for conservative Rathbones clients, or even conservative Rathbones investment managers. The challenge for Adlington is to help managers understand that these investments can provide protection against the ups and downs of stocks and shares. 'Most clients remain largely long of traditional equity, but when you are pitching for new business today you can't just recommend a list of blue chip stocks and trust that this will provide diversification in difficult markets. We must be able to structure a portfolio so that it can perform in any environment. I think that the careful use of alternatives in a diversified portfolio is a better approach than simply relying on stock selection and timing.'

In 2003 Rathbones decided to capitalise on the experience and reputation of its ethical investment team based in Bristol under Elizabeth Haigh, and launched the aptly named Rathbone Greenbank Investments. This business now has over £300m under management, providing a specialist service to more than 500 clients.

The more Rathbones reformed itself, the more it became clear that, under Micky Ingall's and Roy Morris's team, it had a successful formula: the business grew, new clients came, and profits rose steadily. And gradually Rathbones overcame its shyness about blowing its own trumpet. In the mid-1990s, it created a central marketing function to promote the firm more widely in a market that was consolidating and had become hotly competitive. Marketing, business development, brand awareness – all became central to Rathbones' growth strategy. The Rathbones name began to gain currency outside London and Liverpool, though most new client business still came through personal recommendation. Rathbones even began to unbend its austere annual report with pictures and graphs. The 1997 edition listed, for the first time, the size of assets under management in the headline results (£3.3bn of discretionary and £1.2bn of advisory), showing very clearly Rathbones' new measures of success. With the new millennium, the internet added a further dimension to Rathbones' public profile. The firm also began to reach out more, organising events and sponsoring good works which brought publicity. Mark Powell became chairman of the Association of Private Client Investment Managers and Stockbrokers (APCIMS), the trade body.

The installation of the operational nerve centre in Liverpool gave an important boost to Merseyside, which was always in danger of feeling the poor relation as control shifted to London, and assets under management there grew much faster. With this added role, Liverpool took on more space and became a bigger employer than London. This also helped re-establish Rathbones' profile in the city of its birth, where people had come to associate the Rathbone name with a local bakery rather than its oldest financial services company. Rathbones is once again a major local sponsor, particularly of education and the arts, and it was voted Top North West Brand for Professional & Business Services in 2007. Roy Morris became chairman of the Merseyside Partnership in 2000, a public/private venture to boost investment and tourism.

The firm's growth was closely watched by competitors. Mike Burns, who was chief executive of Rensburg Sheppards, the other large independent wealth manager in Liverpool, says that Rathbones was something of a model for his firm: 'We could feel ourselves drifting towards them.' This rapprochement almost bore fruit in 2005 when the two firms considered a merger. But after months of talks, they couldn't agree on a price or a share-out of management positions, and there was a cordial retreat. Some think that merger could still happen.

The changing tone of the firm also required it to decide about its long and colourful history: were all those William Rathbones of yore an asset or a liability? History was good insofar as it spoke of quality and continuity, but bad if it implied clinging to the past. The decision was made to brand the 1742 date because it was distinctive: few firms in Liverpool let alone the City have such a long pedigree. But the

Specialist Schools – as part of Capital of Culture 2008, Rathbones in Liverpool undertook to sponsor four local secondary schools in their bid for Specialist Schools and Academies Trust Status. Shown here are Andy Pomfret, fourth from left, and Andrew Morris, far right, with head teachers from the schools.

accompanying message was that Rathbones was a thoroughly modern firm with its eyes on the future rather than the past. According to Peter Pearson Lund: 'The age of the firm doesn't cut the mustard these days. Many firms succeed without any history at all.' This could be done without hurting feelings: the Rathbone family interest in the company had shrunk to a few per cent and no Rathbone had been involved in management since 1988. The only Rathbone currently working in the business is Julian, the 37-year-old son of Sebastian. He joined having qualified as a chartered accountant with PricewaterhouseCoopers and now heads the Liverpool office's charity team with Rathbones as a whole managing approximately £1bn in charity investments.

The last decade has not, however, been a story of effortless growth. The impressive 22-year run of upward profits came to an end for Rathbones in 2000 when the Wall Street boom in technology stocks crashed, dragging down investment markets all over the world. Rathbones' profits fell from £25m

in 2000 to £18m in 2001 and to £15m the year after that. The crash also knocked half a billion pounds off the value of assets under management. It was the first real test of the management systems installed in the company. Roy Morris, who was chief executive, said it was vital to remain profitable and avoid cutting the dividend. But to do this, costs had to be cut sharply, and there were 19 redundancies – the first that modern Rathbones had ever made. 'We had to strip out costs across the board, nothing was sacred.' But thanks to the greater professionalism and stronger systems that had been instilled into Rathbones' management, the company did succeed in staying profitable through this difficult time, though profits stagnated for three years. It also managed to maintain the dividend but was unable to raise it for a similar period. The re-engineering of the previous years paid off.

When it came, the recovery was swift. In 2005 profits more than doubled to £35m, and assets under management rose strongly again, passing the £10bn mark in 2006. This was helped by a further acquisition from the Belgian bank Dexia of its UK private banking business, including what had been Ely Fund Managers, for £14.5m – and in 2007 profits exceeded £50 million for the first time, despite

Part of a remarkable legacy – Julian Rathbone, son of Sebastian, investment director in Liverpool and William (Bill) Rathbone X who served as a non-executive director on the board from 1994 to 2003.

the liquidity crunch that hit the markets in mid-year.

The recovery period also saw another generation change. Ingall retired as chairman in 2003 and was succeeded by Powell. The following year, Morris retired as well, and Pomfret stepped up to become chief executive. With Chavasse up in Liverpool, Rathbones was now in the hands of a team of people who had no memory of the CFS-Rathbones merger. The transition from partnership to a fully-fledged corporate business was complete.

Next steps

By 2008 Rathbones' new corporate strategy had established it as one of Britain's leading firms in the discretionary private client wealth management business. According to one estimate, it is the third largest, after UBS and Coutts, with the big difference that it is an independent company rather than part of a larger financial conglomerate.*

By then, it had also been in existence for more than two and a half centuries during which time it had mostly prospered, but sometimes come perilously close to disaster – not unusual for a business that lives by its wits. This impressive record owes much to its ability to change with the times, from ships to shares, and more recently from partnership to plc. Even so, much of the firm's strength lies in continuity, a sense of tradition, the human touch. As Mark Powell, the chairman, puts it: 'We have to think in terms of "more of the same".'

Looking ahead, will this enduring business, in the words of William Rathbone VI, be among the swallowers or the swallowed?

This history finds Rathbones in a more settled state than it has been for a long time, with a successful strategy in a flourishing market of growing wealth and sophistication. For professional people, it is also a refuge from the depersonalised mega-banks in the City, one bound together by a strong culture and a respected name.

But in an age where success tends to be measured by numbers rather than the length of corporate histories, Rathbones will face conflicting pressures: to grow without losing the personal touch, to satisfy its shareholders without driving away the human talent which is its most valuable asset. Merger offers may appear, though it is well protected against unfriendly approaches.

Everything is possible for a company which has shown such an impressive ability to adapt and survive, and is determined to claim a future for itself as well as a past.

*Source: Landsbanki estimates, *Private Client Wealth Management Report*, October 2007.

Rathbones usually has two boats at Cowes Week.

Chronology

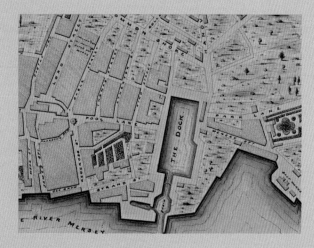

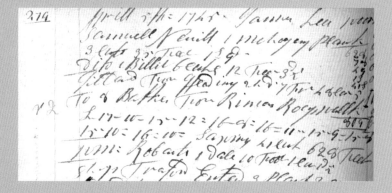

1669	William Rathbone I born in Gawsworth, Cheshire
1688	WRI marries Martha Vigour
1696	WRII is born
1715	Liverpool wet dock is completed
1720	WRII leaves Gawsworth to work in Liverpool
1722	WRII marries Sarah Hyde of Liverpool
1726	WRIII is born in Liverpool
1730	Deed of apprenticeship shows that WRII is in business with Richard Rutter, a Quaker
1731	WRII becomes a Quaker
1732	WRII obtains a lease on property in Hanover St
1739	WRI dies
1741	WRII acquires a further lease in Duke St
	WRII is appointed to renovate the Liverpool Quaker Meeting House
1742	Official date of the foundation of the Rathbones business
1742–47	Surviving Day Book records the growth of the timber business
1746	WRII dies. WRIII takes over and greatly expands the business, trading with America and the Baltic
1750	WRIII marries Rachel Rutter, a fellow Quaker
1754	The completion of the Salthouse Dock adds considerably to Liverpool's port facilities, and provides space for Rathbones' premises at Cornhill
1757	Surviving letter book shows that Rathbones is trading a wide range of commodities, and owns several ships WRIV is born
1768	Evidence that WRIII shipped a slave boy to Lübeck WRIII leases extra land at the Liverpool docks Joseph Rathbone, WRIII's half-brother, marries Mary Darby, cementing ties between the two Quaker families
1780s	Focus of the Rathbones business shifts increasingly towards America after the War of Independence
1783	Rathbones is listed in the Liverpool directory as a plain 'merchant' for the first time, rather than as a 'timber merchant'
1784	WRIII steps back in favour of his son, WRIV Rathbones advertises eight ships sailing to Philadelphia with freight and passengers First trade in cotton

1786	WRIV marries Hannah Mary Reynolds, member of another staunch Quaker family
1787	WRV is born
1788	Richard Rathbone is born The Liverpool Committee for the Abolition of the Slave Trade is set up with Rathbones as members WRIV leases and later buys Greenbank
1789	WRIII dies
1790	Robert Benson joins the Rathbones partnership James Cropper joins as apprentice and becomes partner in 1795
1796	The partnership with Cropper and Benson is dissolved because of Benson's illness WRIV forms a new partnership with William Hughes and William Duncan
1800	WRIV, William Roscoe and other Liverpool reformers form the Friends of Freedom to campaign for social change, peace and the abolition of the slave trade
1801	WRIV and colleagues form the American Chamber of Commerce in Liverpool
1804	WRIV criticises the Quakers and is 'disunited' from the sect
1806	WRV and Richard Rathbone go up to Oxford
1806	Britain blockades Napoleonic ships and ports, severely damaging trade with America. WRIV is strongly opposed to this and organises petitions
1807	The transatlantic slave trade is abolished
1809	WRIV dies WRV and Richard set up their own partnership in competition with Hughes and Duncan
1809–16	Greenbank is rebuilt
1812	WRV marries Elizabeth Greg, forging a link with the Greg cotton textile business. Cotton is growing rapidly in importance for Rathbones
1814	Adam Hodgson joins partnership. He travels widely in America to seek new business opportunities. The firm is renamed Rathbone, Hodgson & Co. The first Rathbones ship sails for India
1817	Richard marries Hannah Mary Reynolds
1818	Rathbones helps inaugurate the first regular passenger sailings to America
1819	WRVI is born at Cornhill

1820–40	Lancashire cotton falls into depression because of a slump in American trade. Rathbones business in the doldrums
1823	Samuel Rathbone is born
1824	Hodgson leaves the firm, which is renamed Rathbone Bros. & Co.
1831	WRV moves into Greenbank, and begins a life of philanthropy and public service
1833	East India Company monopoly on trade with the Far East is abolished
1835	Richard Rathbone retires
1837–8	WRV mayor of Liverpool
1839	WRVI begins his apprenticeship Ross T. Smyth comes to Liverpool from Ireland and forms a grain trading partnership with Rathbones
1840	Rathbones is in serious difficulty. WRV writes: 'We are living hand to mouth'
1842	WRVI joins Rathbones with his younger brother Samuel, and determines that the firm shall be 'among the swallowers, not the swallowed'
1840s	Samuel tours China and sets up branch houses in Canton and Shanghai to deal in silk and tea. WRVI goes to America and develops new contacts. WRVI's scheme of expansion restores the firm's fortunes
1846	Repeal of the Corn Laws opens up the grain trade
1850	Canton and Shanghai houses are closed because of local problems, but the China business continues to thrive through agents
1850s	Shipping interests are evolving. Rathbones becomes one of the largest importers of tea into Britain, and appoints a tea taster in London
1851	Henry Gair is appointed Rathbones agent in New York, and becomes very successful
1852	Rathbones moves its office to Water Street where it remains until 1911 WRVI is told by his father that it is time he went into public service. He enters local politics
1857–63	William Lidderdale succeeds Gair as New York agent
1859	Early death of WRVI's wife, Lucretia Gair. Inspired by the care she received, WRVI founds the district nursing system, with backing from Florence Nightingale
1860	Rathbones opens a London branch

1861	Start of the American Civil War. WRVI freezes trade in cotton on moral and business grounds
1864	Lidderdale becomes a partner, and heads the London office
1868	WRVI is elected MP for Liverpool
1870	Lidderdale becomes a director of the Bank of England
1871	Rathbones pays a record dividend of £80,500 as business recovers after the American Civil War
1881	WRVI is one of the principal founders of University College, Liverpool, which received its Royal Charter in 1881 and became the University of Liverpool in 1903.
1883–4	Business slumps, mainly because of neglect. A partners' review concludes that the firm is not adapting fast enough. A decision is made to sell the cotton business, but the partners fail to agree a new strategy

1889	WRVI retires as partner The shipping business is sold to Harrisons & Crosfield William Lidderdale is appointed Governor of the Bank of England
1890	The Barings crisis
1892	Lidderdale's governorship ends and he returns to Rathbones as a partner
1890s	Rathbones falls into severe decline and heads for crisis
1895	WRVI retires from Parliament
1898	Lidderdale racks up enormous losses in London and retires as partner. The London house is closed 'as quietly as possible' The business is rebuilt in Liverpool with £50,000 of new capital from WRVI and Henry Gair. The focus is to be on husbanding rather than generating wealth

1902	WRVI dies. Management of the firm is taken over by his nephew Robert Rathbone, who loses large amounts of money on wool speculation and in South Africa
1903	Samuel Rathbone dies
1907	WRVI's youngest son Frank takes control of the firm, and relaunches it as a wealth manager
1911	Vere Cotton joins the firm, and becomes its mainstay over the next 50 years
1912	The firm moves to the Royal Liver Building
1934	Frank's son Bertram Lyle (Larry) Rathbone joins the firm

1939	Frank Rathbone dies Larry Rathbone becomes a partner, and Vere Cotton senior partner
1941	The Rathbones office is hit by a bomb and records are destroyed. The business is moved to Castle Street
1944	The Rathbone family completes the transfer of Greenbank to Liverpool University
1960	Vere Cotton retires, Larry becomes senior partner
1960s	The post-war recovery gathers pace
1971	Formation of Comprehensive Financial Services (CFS) in London by Oliver Stanley and colleagues
1982	Larry retires. His cousin Sebastian Rathbone becomes senior partner
1984	CFS goes on to the Unlisted Securities Market (USM) Rathbones moves to the top of the Port of Liverpool building
1988	Rathbones merges with CFS to form Rathbone Brothers Plc. Stanley is chairman, Micky Ingall chief executive
1990s	Sebastian and colleagues retire. Acquisition of new businesses and investment teams from other firms using Ingall formula fuels rapid expansion
1992	Rathbones shares are admitted to the Official List. Celebration of 250 years since the start of the Day Book
1995	Acquisition of Laurence Keen
1996	Acquisition of Neilson Cobbold
1997	Stanley retires and is succeeded as chairman by Ingall. Roy Morris becomes chief executive Move to 159 New Bond Street, London
1999	Formation of Rathbone Unit Trust Management Andy Pomfret joins firm as finance director
2000	Twenty two-year record of unbroken profits growth is ended by the dotcom market crash.
2001	Paul Chavasse joins the firm and becomes chief operating officer
2003	Ingall retires and is succeeded by Mark Powell
2004	Morris retires as chief executive and is succeeded by Andy Pomfret
2006	Acquisition of Dexia's UK private banking business for £14.5m. Funds under management exceed £10bn for the first time
2007	Profits exceed £50m for the first time.

Bibliography and sources

In writing this book, I drew on a wide range of primary and secondary sources.

Secondary sources are often the best starting point, and I began with Lucie Nottingham's excellent *Rathbone Brothers. From Merchant to Banker 1742–1992*, which was published by Rathbone Brothers in 1992 and covered the period from the earliest days up to the (then) recent merger with CFS. Another valuable study was Sheila Marriner's *Rathbones of Liverpool 1845–73*, published by the Liverpool University Press in 1961, which gives an intensive insight into the heyday of Rathbones as a merchant/shipping company.

The Rathbones themselves were also prodigious chroniclers of their history, and their writings provided a rich source of primary material: letters, essays, diaries, books on which I drew heavily for information and quotes. Chief among these is *A Sketch of Family History* compiled by William Rathbone VI and published privately in 1894. This was later amplified by his daughter Eleanor Rathbone in her *William Rathbone: A Memoir* published by Macmillan & Co. in 1905, and by *Records of the Rathbone Family* compiled by Emily Rathbone and published privately in 1913. The three works tend to overlap and retell the more colourful stories in Rathbones' history, but all are enriched by personal memoir and can be treated as primary sources as well. A further source of family memoirs is *Reynolds-Rathbone Diaries and Letters 1753–1839* edited by Elizabeth Eustace Greg and published privately in 1905.

The main documentary sources are the Rathbone Papers in the Special Collections and Archives of the Sydney Jones Library, University of Liverpool, and the private collections of the Rathbone family, to which I was given access and found invaluable. Many of the earlier documents quoted in this book came from these sources.

Additional sources of Rathbone family history included Joy Robinson's *Relatively Rathbone* (Trotman and Co. 1992), a delightful account of family life and personalities, and Adrian Allan's *Greenbank, A Brief History* (University of Liverpool 1987). Given the importance of the Quakers to this story, I also consulted Paul Emden's *Quakers in Commerce* (Sampson Low 1939).

The story of Rathbones cannot be disconnected from that of Liverpool, and here I was fortunate to be able to draw on the excellent work produced by the University of Liverpool to mark the City's 800th anniversary in 2007, in particular *Liverpool 800: Culture, Character and History*, edited by John Belchem and published by the Liverpool University Press in 2006. For additional material about shipping I used Robin Gardiner's *The History of the White Star Line* (Ian Allan 2001).

For information about the London connection, particularly William Lidderdale's governorship of the Bank of England, I drew on David Kynaston's *The City of London* (Chatto & Windus 1994), and the Lidderdale files in the Bank of England archives.

DL

Adrian Allan, *Greenbank, A Brief History*, University of Liverpool 1987

David Kynaston, *The City of London*, Chatto & Windus 1994

Eleanor Rathbone, *William Rathbone: A Memoir*, Macmillan & Co. 1905

Emily Rathbone (ed.), *Records of the Rathbone Family*, private publication 1913

John Belchem (ed.), *Liverpool 800: Culture, Character and History*, Liverpool University Press 2006

Joy Robinson, *Relatively Rathbone*, Trotman and Co. 1992

Lucie Nottingham, *Rathbone Brothers. From Merchant to Banker 1742–1992*, Rathbone Brothers Plc 1992

Paul Emden, *Quakers in Commerce*, Sampson Low 1939

Robin Gardiner, *The History of the White Star Line*, Ian Allan 2001

Sheila Marriner, *Rathbones of Liverpool 1845–73*, Liverpool University Press 1961

William Rathbone VI, *A Sketch of Family History*, private publication 1894

Index

Page numbers in *italics* indicate illustrations.

Acknowledgements

Many people contributed to this book with interviews, information and guidance covering more than 300 years of Rathbone family and business records.

In particular I would like to mention – at present-day Rathbones – Hugh Adlington, Mary Armitage, Rupert Baron, Ian Buckley, Paul Chavasse, Giles Coode-Adams, Elizabeth Haigh, Andrew Hutton, Brian Kenny, Paul Loughlin, Richard Loader, Richard Lanyon, Emily Morris, Peter Pearson Lund, Andy Pomfret, Mark Powell, Julian Rathbone and Julie Williams.

From Rathbones of yore and CFS, my thanks to Anthony Furse, Micky Ingall, John Leigh, Roy Morris, Anthony Nottingham and Oliver Stanley for their memories. It was kind of Mike Burns, formerly of Rensburg Sheppards, to contribute a competitor's view of Rathbones. I am also grateful to Sue Rathbone, Anthony Rathbone, the Rev. Steve Rathbone and Cledwyn Thomas for information about the Rathbone family. My thanks go to Anthony and Hilda Gaddum for an introduction to Gawsworth.

My research was greatly assisted by Lucie Nottingham, author of an earlier history of Rathbones, and Katy Hooper and her colleagues who look after the Rathbone Papers in the Special Collections at the Sydney Jones Library at the University of Liverpool. I am also indebted to Sarah Millard at the Bank of England Archives for permission to go through the Lidderdale files.

I reserve special thanks for William Rathbone X whose support for this project and generosity with sources and material are enormously appreciated.
DL

Publisher's credits

James & James would like to thank Adrian Allan and Katy Hooper at the University of Liverpool for their generous help and meticulous checking of the proofs, Roger Hull at the Liverpool Record Office and Johanna Booth at National Museums Liverpool for researching and supplying images, William Rathbone X for kindly providing material, Clive and Fiona Henderson for allowing themselves to be photographed during a meeting and a special thanks to Charles Best for his superb modern pictures and his calm good humour throughout. The publisher is also indebted to Emily Morris for her management of the project for Rathbones and Tabitha Wrathall for her help in Liverpool.

James & James would like to thank the following for supplying images:
©**Alamy**: 15 (left), 112, Alan Novelli, 15 (right) Ed Rhodes, 62 North Wind Picture Archives, 87 (bottom) John Rendle NZ, 109 Pictorial Press Ltd, 112(top) David Moore, 119 (top) Terry Fincher/Photo International, 119 (bottom) John Sturrock ©**Athenaeum Club**: 25 photo by John Hammond **Charles Best**: 2, 6, 10, 14, 16, 28, 40, 60, 69 (bottom left), 72, 78, 88 (bottom), 90, 94, 101 (bottom), 106 (top), 107 (top), 110, 114, 122 (below), 124, 126, 127, 129, 130, 131 ©**The Bridgeman Art Library**: 26 Private Collection, Photo Christie's Images, 34 Yale Center for British Art, Paul Mellon Collection, USA, 35, 37 Wilberforce House, Hull City Museums and Art Galleries, UK, 36 Library of Congress, Washington D.C., USA, 41 Ironbridge Gorge Museum, Telford, Shropshire, UK, 45, 66, 75 Private Collection, The Stapleton Collection, 47 Bibliotheque Nationale, Paris, France, Giraudon, 49 (right), 65, 75 Private Collection, 49 (bottom right) The Royal Institution, London UK, 58, 59 University of Liverpool Art Gallery & Collections, UK, 81 David David Gallery, Philadelphia, PA, USA ©**Martin Charles**: 54, 113 (top right) ©**Corbis**: 48 C. Gianni Dagli Orti, 96, 113 (top left) Richard Klune, 122 (top) Pawel Libera **James Cropper**: 91 (bottom) **David Gentleman**: 116 **Imperial War Museum, London**: 105 (bottom) ©**Kos/kospictures.com**: 132 **Liverpool Record Office, Liverpool Libraries**: 12, 20, 22, 27, 31, 32 Herdman Collection, 84, 85 (top) Herdman Collection, 85 (bottom), 86 (left), 91 (top) ©**MaddieDigitalPhotography**: 8, 56 **Mary Evans**: 64, 87 (top), 95, 101 (top), 102 **National Maritime Museum, Greenwich, London**: 28, 83 ©**National Museums Liverpool**: 14, 89 Maritime Museum, 103 Sudley House, 29, 50 Walker Art Gallery ©**National Portrait Gallery, London**: 38 ©**National Trust Photo Library**: 63, 105 (top) Chambré Hardman Archive **Private Collections**: 56, 74, 80, 106 (bottom), 107 (bottom), 108 (top) 117 **William Rathbone X**: 19, 24, 26, 47, 63, 67, 86 (right), 93, 96, 100, 104 **The Royal School for the Blind, Liverpool**: 49 (bottom) **Oliver Stanley**: 116, 121, 138 **University of Liverpool Special Collection and Archives**: 18, 42, 43, 51, 57, 68, 70, 73, 88, 92, 99, 108, 109, 120.